VIEN

A Complete Musical Guide

GUY HARTOPP

FAXTON
music publications

© 2006 Guy Hartopp
Vienna - a Complete Musical Guide

ISBN 0-9551480-0-6

Published by
Faxton Music Publications
Market Harborough
LE16 8NE

A CIP catalogue record of this book
can be obtained from the British Library.

Design & production co-ordinated by:
The Better Book Company Ltd
Havant
Hampshire
PO9 2XH

Printed in England

Cover design by MusicPrint, Chichester

TABLE OF CONTENTS

PREFACE

This book is intended for lovers of music who have been drawn to Vienna by the city's incomparable musical heritage. So many of the great composers were either born in Vienna or chose to live there. Even more made their musical mark on the city during extended visits.

While preparing this book a number of difficulties presented themselves. Firstly there was the sheer size of the task. Secondly there was the problem of what to include in a book claiming to be a "complete musical guide". For example, the sanatorium in which Gustav Mahler died is rightly included, but only the most committed Mahlerian will be interested in the clinic where he underwent surgery for haemorrhoids.

A number of entries begin with the depressing words: "the present building stands on the site of ......". In the Innere Stadt particularly, many buildings of immense musical significance no longer exist or have been modified substantially. The closing days of the Second World War, in which much of the centre of Vienna was laid waste, had a devastating effect upon the city's musical sites.

Although these sites will be of interest mainly to the music scholar, had they been omitted, this account of the musical life of Vienna would have been distorted and incomplete. The aim of this book is not simply to provide a list of which composer lived where and when. Where possible background information has been given to place each entry in its historical context and to add to the interest of the reader.

Occasional passages in italics represent an opinion or observation of the author, who takes responsibility for any errors and omissions.

Often it will be necessary to use public transport, and therefore a brief guide to the public transport system of Vienna is given below.

To visit every place of musical interest in Vienna will require a number of visits. I can assure the reader that the attraction of this city will never pall.

Guy Hartopp

PUBLIC TRANSPORT IN VIENNA

Public transport in Vienna is efficient, frequent, clean and reasonably priced. The most economic use is by means of a 3- or 5- day ticket. Tickets are available at the U–Bahn stations and also at "Tabak" – tobacconist shops. They are valid for trams, buses and the underground trains.

All bus and tram stops are named and the next stop announced over the intercom. A map of the route of each bus and tram is displayed in the vehicle, and on the U–Bahn.

All routes and stops are marked on most maps of the city. For more detailed information a comprehensive map of Viennese transport, including the rapid transit train system to outlying villages such as Mödling, is available at the Karlsplatz U–Bahn Station.

There are no conductors on board trams or buses. With either a single or period ticket all that is required is to enter the ticket into one of the blue machines placed by the doors of trams and buses and at the entrance to U–Bahn stations. A "ping" confirms that the ticket has been stamped. For period tickets no further franking is necessary. Always carry the ticket when making a journey; checks are few and far between but they do occur and travelling without a valid ticket is an offence not taken lightly in Vienna.

ACKNOWLEDGEMENTS

The principal sources of this book are to be found in the bibliography. There are some, however, who are deserving of special mention, notably O.E. Deutsch. His "Documentary Biographies" of Schubert and Mozart are astonishing *tours de force*.

The Haydn and Mozart scholar H.C. Robbins-Landon is essential reading for anyone interested in music in Vienna. Robbins-Landon's scholarship, while being beyond question, is presented with a light touch and is eminently readable.

Henry-Louis de la Grange's meticulously researched multi-volume biography of Mahler is a fund of information about that composer.

Rudolf Klein undertook the task of cataloguing Beethoven's places of residence, (there were over 40).

My thanks also to Dr. Robert Waissenberger, formerly Director of the Museen der Stadt Wien, and his colleagues who patiently responded to every query, however minor.

My grateful thanks to Joan Coster and Cheryl McCarthy who accomplished the near-impossible task of deciphering my handwriting and typed the script.

Finally, to my wife Carolyn for her patient and always constructive criticism.

For Carolyn, Richard and Kathryn.
And Jim McClurg; this book was
written at his suggestion

I St. Stephen's Cathedral

St. Stephen's cathedral is the most familiar landmark in Vienna. It has stood in silent witness to eight centuries of Viennese history. This imposing edifice survived, relatively unscathed, furious bombardments by the Turks and the French before succumbing to intense incendiary bombing in the closing days of the Second World War. After the war the cathedral was rebuilt and it remains the geographical and spiritual centre of Vienna.

St. Stephen's has a rich musical history; it has been served by a distinguished line of *Domkapellmeister* and, in differing ways, it has played a part in the lives (and deaths) of a number of composers as the following examples illustrate:-

Haydn

Franz Joseph Haydn became a boy chorister at St. Stephen's in 1740 at the age of eight and remained there until his eighteenth year. The choirboys were housed in spartan accommodation in the "Kantor-Haus", which stood close to the cathedral on the south side. (It was demolished at the turn of the nineteenth century).

Haydn received sound instruction in the art of singing, and also in playing the klavier and the violin, but none in music theory or composition. The older and more gifted choirboys were expected to teach the younger ones; thus in due course Joseph taught his younger brother Michael Haydn, who in turn instructed the youngest of the Haydn brothers, Peter. (Michael became a fine and prolific composer in his own right. For 40 years he was Kapellmeister to the Archbishop of Salzburg, where he was on good terms with the Mozart family).

Discipline was strict; both Joseph and Michael recalled ruefully the regular canings meted out by the Domkapellmeister Georg Reutter. The busy schedule of the choir left little time for normal academic subjects, which were neglected.

The choirboys were also in demand for secular activities at the palaces of the aristocracy, including Schönbrunn Palace (see XVI:3). These occasions were eagerly anticipated by the boys. The reward for the performance was usually a plate of cakes which made a welcome change from the sparse fare offered at the choir school.

Two stories relating to Haydn's departure from the choir should be treated with a degree of caution. One account is of Haydn cutting off the "queue" of a fellow chorister; he was given a thrashing for the offence, and then expelled.

Even less credence should be given to a story related in a biography of Haydn by Georg Griesinger, a minor diplomat who befriended Haydn late in the composer's life. According to this tale, Kapellmeister Reutter planned to extend Haydn's career as a soprano indefinitely by means of a small surgical operation, rendering Haydn a castrato, a plan thwarted only by the timely arrival of Haydn's father. There is no corroborative evidence to support this story.

The simple and harsh truth is that when the boys' voices broke, they were obliged to leave the choir without means. For Haydn this meant a short period of genuine privation. (see V: 23).

On November 26th 1760, Haydn returned to St. Stephen's to marry Maria Anna Kellner, the daughter of a barber and wig-maker. Haydn was 28 and his bride 32. For Haydn it would prove to be a deeply unhappy as well as childless marriage. Maria was hot-tempered, ill-educated and a spendthrift. She preferred the company of clerics, dogs and cats to that of her husband, and had no interest in his musical career. Even Haydn, always reticent about his private life, was moved to complain that "she has no redeeming virtues; it is a matter of indifference to her whether I am an artist or an artisan". Nevertheless, Haydn remained married to Maria until her death forty years later, although he took care to see as little of her as possible.

Maria and her younger sister Theresia were piano students of Haydn. He fell in love with Theresia, but she, either by personal inclination or family pressure, decided to become a nun and joined the convent of St. Nicolas (see III: 3). For reasons that have remained unclear, Haydn made the cardinal mistake of marrying her elder sister. Although he remained married to Maria, by his own admission he sought female companionship elsewhere. "My wife was unable to bear children, therefore I was not indifferent to the charms of other women".

Fux

In 1741 in St. Stephen's, there took place the funerals of two composers in both of which it is probable, although never ascertained, that the young Haydn took part. The first, in February of that year, was of the Hofkapellmeister, composer and theorist Johann Fux. He was the author of a learned treatise on counterpoint, Gradus ad Parnassum. Haydn, largely self-taught as a composer, prized his copy of this treatise highly, and worked on the exercises diligently.

Vivaldi

The other notable funeral of 1741 was that of Antonio Vivaldi on July 28th. Vivaldi had died of "internal inflammation" at the house of a saddler, which stood approximately on the site of the Staatsoper. The 9-year old Haydn was probably one of the six choirboys who sang his Requiem Mass.

In 1740 the "Red Priest" travelled from Venice to Vienna to seek fame and fortune in the Austrian capital. In Venice interest in his music had declined sharply, and the church authorities there were suspicious and disapproving of the nature of his relationship with the singer Anna Girò. Vivaldi made no impression on Vienna and he died in poverty.

Mozart

On the 4th August 1782 in St. Stephen's cathedral Wolfgang Amadeus Mozart married Constanza Weber. Mozart was 26 and his wife six years his junior. Like Haydn, Mozart married the sister of a woman who had rejected him. (Mozart had been infatuated with Constanza's older sister Aloysia). In a letter to his father Leopold in Salzburg, Mozart described the ceremony. "The only persons present were Constanza's mother and younger sister (Sophie), the sisters' guardian and two friends. When we were joined together both my bride and I shed tears. All present, even the priest, were much moved, and all wept at witnessing these tokens of our deep emotion".

The emotions that Leopold felt on receiving this letter were those of anger and despair. Leopold's distrust of the Weber family was profound and he was appalled when news of Mozart's developing relationship with Constanza reached him. His paternal blessing for the union, granted with the utmost reluctance, arrived too late for the ceremony.

To the long line of worthy "Domkapellmeister" would have been added the name of Mozart, had the composer lived a little longer. In April 1791, seven months before his death, Mozart applied for the post of assistant Kapellmeister without remuneration. This position was in the gift of the Municipal Council of Vienna. Mozart's obsequious petition to the Council was eventually accepted, and Mozart became the assistant (unpaid) to the incumbent Kapellmeister Leopold Hofmann, who at the time was seriously ill.

Mozart's clear intention was to succeed Hofmann as Domkapellmeister at St. Stephen's, a position which carried a comfortable salary. It would have enabled Mozart to discharge his debts and his family to enjoy a decent standard of living. In the event Mozart predeceased Hofmann, and Johann Albrechtsberger secured the post in 1792.

Franz Xaver Wolfgang Mozart was baptised in St. Stephen's on July 26th 1791. Wolfgang junior was the sixth and last of the Mozarts' children, and one of only two to survive infancy.

Wolfgang junior also became a musician, receiving lessons from both Antonio Salieri and Albrechtsberger. Unfortunately his compositions revealed a small talent and he earned his living as a teacher of the piano. He remained unmarried, and died at the age of 53 in Karlsbad (today called Karlovy Vary).

In December 1791 Mozart returned to St. Stephen's – in his coffin. He died at five minutes to one on the morning of December 5th 1791. The circumstances surrounding the funeral of Mozart have been shrouded in mystery for two centuries. It is not known for certain who attended and it is unclear whether the obsequies were held inside the cathedral or in an outside chapel. Even the date has been brought into question.

The distinguished Mozart scholar H.C. Robbins-Landon has compiled an account of the probable sequence of events which is in accord with parish records and with the consensus of opinion among other scholars:-

At approximately 3pm on the afternoon of December 6th 1791 a funeral wagon carried Mozart's coffin from his last residence in the Rauhensteingasse (see II: 10) to the cathedral. The coffin was placed on a bier in the "Capistranus pulpit" on the north side of the cathedral for the first blessing. It was then carried inside the cathedral, probably through the "Bishop's Gate", and into the Kreuzkapelle where the mourners were waiting. The Kreuzkapelle is a small intimate chapel situated beneath the Heidenturm just inside the main entrance on the left.

Among those believed to be present were:-

Johann Albrechtsberger
Franz Süssmayer (Mozart's pupil)
Antonio Salieri (Hofkapellmeister)
Baron Gottfried von Swieten (Mozart's patron and friend
    who made the funeral arrangements)
Joseph Lang
       } Mozart's brothers-in-law
Franz Hofer
Joseph Deiner (a waiter at a local inn which Mozart
    frequented during the last few months of his life)
Also two or three members of the orchestra of the Theater auf
    der Wieden. Constanza did not attend.

After the brief service the coffin was carried out of the cathedral and returned to the "Capistranus pulpit" for the final blessing. It was then lifted on to the funeral wagon in readiness for its final journey to the cemetery of St. Marx (see XVII : A).

Much of the confusion and controversy about the Mozart's funeral emanated from a "memoir", purportedly by Joseph Deiner, which appeared in a Viennese newspaper, the "Morgen-post" in January 1856 to mark the centenary of Mozart's birth. Robbins-Landon has described this article as "one of the greatest frauds in Mozart scholarship".

In his account, Deiner asserts that the funeral was held on December 7th rather than the 6th, and that the entire proceedings took place in the "Capistranus pulpit". This tiny chapel has no access to the interior of the cathedral. At the rear of the chapel there is a staircase leading down to the crypt.

But it is Deiner's description of the weather, which has given rise to serious doubts as to the authenticity of the "memoir". "... at the funeral it began to rage and storm. Rain and snow fell at the same time, as if Nature wanted to show her anger with the great composer's contemporaries, who had turned out extremely sparsely for his burial".

Purple prose of this quality would only be acceptable if the contents were factually correct. According to meteorological records, December 6th was calm, mild and slightly misty. On December 7th, a cold gusty wind arose in the late afternoon, albeit with no precipitation. Dr. Carl Bär has tried to reconcile Deiner's account with the known facts by suggesting that the parish records are incorrect, and that the funeral took place on December 7th. In his admirable and thoroughly researched treatise on Mozart's death and burial, Bär cites the statutory regulation of the time which required that 48 hours should elapse between death and burial. This was a compromise between the fear of being buried alive, and the understandable desire to dispose of the corpse before the onset of putrefaction.

At the rear of the Capistranus pulpit, a commemorative plaque marks the event: "Here the mortal remains of the immortal W.A. Mozart were blessed; December 6th 1791". The date on the plaque corresponds with that given in the Register of Deaths of the Parish of St. Stephen's.

Deiner's memoir has coloured biographers' accounts of Mozart's death and funeral ever since. The author can offer only one hypothesis to explain its contradictions: that "Joseph Deiner" was an enterprising journalist indulging in an early example of "historical fiction". By assuming the persona of the mourner least known to subsequent generations, and embellishing known facts with elements of romantic fiction, the writer of the article added a sense of immediacy and drama to one of the most poignant episodes of musical history.

Chopin

Over the centuries the majestic splendour of St. Stephen's has given inspiration and consolation to many, but it failed to dispel the gloomy mood of Frédéric Chopin in 1830. Chopin was paying his second visit to Vienna, one which was proving markedly less successful than his first.

Lonely and depressed about his professional prospects in the Austrian capital, Chopin went to St. Stephen's for midnight mass at Christmas 1830.

In a letter to a friend, Chopin described his feelings as he entered the cathedral: "A tomb behind me, a tomb below me, it only needed a tomb above me .... I felt my loneliness more keenly than ever".

Johann Strauss (father)

Johann Strauss (father) died on September 25th 1849 at the age of 45. Two days later St. Stephen's was full as his coffin was borne into the cathedral on the shoulders of members of the Strauss orchestra. Thousands more stood in silent tribute outside.

Johann Strauss (son)

In August 1862 the younger Johann Strauss married Henriette ("Jetti") Chalupetzky in St. Stephen's cathedral. The announcement of their engagement had prompted deep misgivings in the Strauss family, and raised eyebrows among the Viennese. Not only was she, at 44, seven years older than Strauss, she had also previously given birth to no fewer than seven illegitimate children. After a successful career as a mezzo-soprano she retired and became the mistress of a wealthy Viennese banker.

The family's doubts were soon allayed. Jetti proved the ideal wife for her highly-strung husband. She lifted the administrative burden from Strauss and, with her musical background, was a considerable help in the correction and copying of scores. It is Jetti who has been given the credit for persuading Strauss to withdraw from the frenetic world of performing in dance halls, and to turn to the composition of operettas.

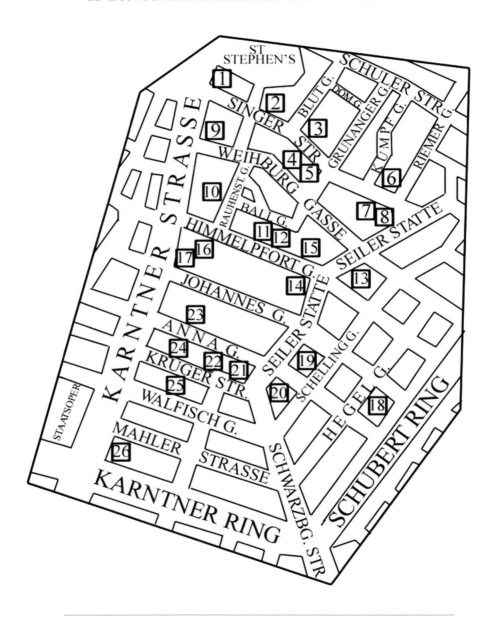

I Singerstrasse 3

Salieri

The Hotel Royal stands on the site of a former residence of Antonio Salieri. Born in Legnago in Italy, Salieri came to Vienna as a young man to study under Gluck and Gassmann, who he succeeded as Court Composer in 1774. When in 1788, he was appointed Hofkapellmeister, he became one of the most powerful musical figures in Vienna.

It was towards the end of his life, after a sad decline into senility, that Salieri is alleged to have confessed to poisoning Mozart. (see XII: 9). Within five years, Pushkin had produced his one-act play "Mozart and Salieri", later turned into an eminently forgettable opera by Rimsky-Korsakov.

But it is Peter Schaffer's play and film "Amadeus" which has tarnished, probably irretrievably, the reputation of Antonio Salieri. In "Amadeus" Salieri, a worthy mediocrity, rails against divine injustice when he realises that genius has been bestowed upon Mozart, caricatured in the film as an infantile buffoon with a predilection for scatological humour.

Salieri was not a mediocre composer; He composed over forty operas and much choral and instrumental music. The best of Salieri's music has melodic grace and freshness of invention and deserves to be better known.

Salieri was also highly esteemed as a teacher. Beethoven turned to him when lessons with Haydn proved unsatisfactory. Salieri taught Beethoven the art of vocal writing in the Italian style (not altogether successfully). Salieri both recognised and nurtured the precocious talent of Schubert (see III: 9). He also numbered among his pupils Liszt, Hummel and Wolfgang Mozart Junior.

After two centuries it is perhaps time for a reappraisal of Salieri's music and his considerable contribution to the musical life of Vienna.

I Singerstrasse 7, The Deutschordenshaus

Mozart

In March 1781 Archbishop Colloredo of Salzburg, Mozart's employer, was staying at the Deutschordenshaus with a full complement of courtiers and servants, including musicians. Mozart, who had been granted an extended leave of absence by the Archbishop for the première of *Idomeneo* in Munich, was summoned to Vienna.

On arrival he found himself ensconced with the other servants. His rebellious frame of mind is evident in a sarcastic letter to his father in Salzburg. "We eat at midday ... I am seated below the valets, but I at least have the honour to sit above the cooks".

Musical entertainment was required daily. Among the works that Mozart composed for these "house concerts"was the Violin Sonata in G (K379), written between 11pm and midnight on the night before the concert. Particularly galling for Mozart was the refusal of the Archbishop to allow him to take part in a concert which would have realised a sum equivalent to half his annual salary. Colloredo also forbade Mozart to take part in a charity concert at the Kärntnertor Theatre, although peer pressure persuaded the Archbishop to change his mind, and Mozart enjoyed a major success.

The deteriorating relationship between Mozart and the Archbishop is chronicled in Mozart's letters to a horrified Leopold, who no doubt was concerned about his own position in the Archbishop's service. Matters came to a head when Mozart was ordered to return to Salzburg. Mozart employed delaying tactics to prolong his stay in Vienna. There followed an altercation, in the course of which Colloredo called Mozart a "scoundrel" and a "vagabond". Seething with self-righteous indignation, Mozart submitted his formal resignation which Count Carl Arco, chamberlain to the Archbishop, calmly refused to accept. He counselled Mozart to be less intemperate, and also gave him some sound advice: "Do not allow yourself to be dazzled by Vienna. At first you are overwhelmed with praise, ... but soon the Viennese want something new". Mozart would have cause to recall this advice a few years later.

Mozart then submitted his resignation again, this time with no response from Count Arco. Arco was an even-tempered man who had always been well-disposed towards the Mozarts. But when Mozart approached him for the third time, Arco lost both his patience and his temper, and ended Mozart's employment with a hefty kick on the composer's backside.

History, rather unfairly, has assigned to Colloredo the role of villain of the piece. Although the Archbishop was a member of the "ancien régime" with a deserved reputation as a martinet, he was not considered unjust or unfair. That the equable-tempered Count Arco should so lose his self-control that he offered physical violence to Mozart suggests that, on this occasion, Mozart's behaviour left something to be desired.

Brahms

Between 1863 and 1865, Johannes Brahms stayed at the Deutschordenshaus occupying three small rooms on the fourth floor. Brahms was the musical director of the Singakadamie, founded eight years before by a group of amateurs with a love of early ecclesiastical music and, in particular, of *a capella* singing. It gave four concerts annually, the last of which was a major oratorio for which the choir engaged an orchestra. Musical standards had slipped and the choir looked to Brahms to improve matters. But Brahms found the task too onerous and resigned after one season.

At thirty, Brahms was beginning to make his mark on Vienna as a composer. During his stay at the Deutschordenshaus, he was occupied by the Cello Sonata in E minor, the String Sextet in G, the Trio for Horn, Violin and Piano Op.40 and the Sonata for two pianos which metamorphosed into the great Piano Quintet, Op.34.

It was at the Deutschordenshaus in February 1865 that Brahms received news of the serious illness of his mother. He hastened to her bedside in Hamburg only to discover that she had died. Deeply saddened by her death, Brahms began to make preliminary sketches for a work which, after a lengthy gestation period, became "A German Requiem". With this noble work, Brahms would be universally acknowledged as a master.

Beethoven, Schubert

In the first half of the nineteenth century, this building was the Café Bogner, a coffee-house much frequented by both Beethoven and the Schubert circle of friends. Bogner's became favourite haunt of Schubert in 1826 and remained so until his death in 1828. Schubert and his friends often arrived at the café after spending an evening carousing in a nearby tavern. In the more tranquil atmosphere of the coffee-house they would talk until the early hours of the morning.

In the entrance to Bogner's was a life-size drawing of a Turkish man. It had been executed by one of Schubert's friends, the artist Moritz von Schwind, apparently in lieu of settlement of his account.

In 1828 while on his deathbed (see IX: 14), Schubert requested a friend to acquire novels by James Fennimore Cooper and to deposit them at Bogner's for collection.

4   I Singerstrasse 18

Schubert

This house was the home of the four talented Fröhlich sisters. (They later moved to the Spiegelgasse). The eldest, Anna, was a teacher of singing at the Conservatoire and the second sister Barbara, an artist. The two younger sisters, Katharine and Josefine had beautiful singing voices.

The sisters held open house for all lovers of music, and from 1820 Schubert was a regular guest. Here Schubert became acquainted with Franz Grillparzer, the poet and dramatist. Grillparzer had developed an abiding passion for Katharine, the most attractive of the sisters, although he could never bring himself to marry her.

Schubert composed his beautiful setting of Psalm 23 for female voices for Anna's students at the Conservatoire. In 1828 Schubert gave his only public concert of his own music. At this concert, Anna conducted Josefine and the lady pupils of the Conservatoire in Schubert's setting of Grillparzer's poem *Ständchen* (D920).

5   I Singerstrasse 22

Albrechtsberger

This house was the final residence of Johann Albrechtsberger; he died here in 1809. He succeeded Mozart as assistant Kapellmeister at St. Stephen's, becoming Domkapellmeister in 1792. A prolific though unremarkable composer, Albrechtsberger is best remembered as a theorist and teacher. He numbered among his pupils Beethoven, Hummel and Wolfgang Mozart junior. Beethoven's awareness of the deficiencies in his musical knowledge is apparent from the countless turgid contrapuntal exercises to which he subjected himself under Albrechtsberger's guidance. Albrechtsberger was clearly unimpressed by Beethoven's early compositions. On being shown a new quartet by his former pupil he declared: "Beethoven learned nothing from me; he will never be any good!"

6   I Singerstrasse 21

Johann Strauss (son)

On this site stood an apartment building in which Johann Strauss (son) and his new bride Jetti (see I) lived for a few months in 1862-3. It was during his stay here that Strauss applied for a third time for the title, "K.K. Hofball-Musik –Direktor", which had previously been conferred upon his late father. His first two applications had been refused by the Emperor on the advice of the police authorities, which were mindful of the activities of Strauss during the 1848 revolution. Strauss had sided with the insurgents, composing such works as "The Revolutionary March", and had received a police reprimand for playing the *Marseillaise* at a concert.

But fifteen years had elapsed since the revolution and the authorities, aware of the increasing popularity of Strauss, and optimistic that his new marriage was indicative of growing maturity, raised no objection. The Emperor thus conferred upon Strauss the title that he had coveted.

I Singerstrasse 28

Zu den drei Hacken

"The Three Hatchets" was a favourite inn of Schubert and his friends. A plaque refers to some of the guests who foregathered for lunch at this tavern. Apart from that of Schubert himself the names of Franz von Schober and Moritz von Schwind are also recorded.

8 **I Singerstrasse 32**

Wagner

The apartment house that stood on this site was the residence of Dr Josef Standhartner, chief medical officer at the General Hospital, personal physician to the Empress Elizabeth and an avowed Wagnerian. In 1861 Wagner was in Vienna seeking to stage the première of *Tristan und Isolde*. With his family away on holiday, Dr Standhartner was able to offer accommodation, and for several weeks Wagner was a house guest of his admirer. Plans for *Tristan* did not progress well. The singers complained that the music was too difficult and the opera was deemed unperformable. Wagner's attitude towards Vienna was always ambivalent and his initial optimism rapidly changed to frustration and despair. His attempt to stage *Tristan* in Vienna eventually proved fruitless. When Dr. Standhartner's family returned from holiday, Wagner moved to the Hotel Kaiserin Elizabeth (see II: 9) which the impecunious composer could ill-afford.

9 **I Weihberggasse 3**

Mozart

In September 1787 the Mozart family lodged with a goldsmith in a house which stood on this site. Leopold Mozart hoped that eleven-year-old Wolfgang would be invited to perform during the festivities on the occasion of a Royal wedding. Leopold's plans went awry when a smallpox epidemic claimed the life of the bride-to-be, a daughter of Empress Maria Theresa. Leopold rapidly removed his family from Vienna, but it was too late. Both the Mozart children contracted smallpox. Of the two, Wolfgang was the more severely affected and, on recovery, the characteristic pockmarks of the disease were evident.

Hotel Kaiserin Elizabeth

Since the early nineteenth century the site has been occupied by the Hotel Kaiserin Elizabeth. A plaque in the foyer records some of its distinguished guests including Clara Schumann, Liszt, Wagner, Bruckner, Anton Rubinstein and Grieg. (For reasons best known to the management " Mozart 1767" (see above) also appears on the plaque).

Edvard Grieg visited Vienna in 1896, staying at the Hotel Kaiserin Elizabeth. Grieg became very friendly with Brahms; Grieg recalled fondly the evenings they spent together in local inns. Brahms appreciated the Norwegian composer's use of the folksongs of his homeland. When Grieg developed a severe attack of bronchitis Brahms, with uncharacteristic solicitude, paid no less than three visits here to enquire about his friend's health.

10   I Rauhensteingasse 8

In an apartment house that stood on this site Mozart died in December 1791. The house was demolished in 1847 and replaced by the "Mozarthof" which was in turn superseded by a department store. The commemorative plaque on the rear of the store is an unsatisfactory and unworthy memorial to one of the greatest geniuses of all time.

The Mozarts had occupied the apartment since September 1790. Among the works that he composed here were the Piano Concerto No. 27 in B♭ (K595), the Clarinet Concerto in A (K622), *La Clemenza di Tito* and "The Magic Flute".

In July 1791 the Mozart's last child Franz Xaver Wolfgang was born here.

In the same month a mysterious stranger, dressed in grey, presented himself at Mozart's apartment with a commission for a Requiem Mass. The fee was to be very generous with the proviso that the composer of the work should be anonymous. The stranger was a steward of a certain Count Walsegg-Stupach who planned to pass off the Requiem, in memory of his late wife, as his own work. Mozart, working overtime to complete his last two operas, became increasingly concerned about the frequent visits of the steward who was demanding news of progress of the Requiem.

Mozart died on December 5th 1791 with the work unfinished. Constanza eventually asked Mozart's pupil Franz Süssmayer to complete the Requiem.

The cause of Mozart's death

Death by poisoning has all but been discounted by Mozart scholars. A detailed discussion of the medical aspects of Mozart's death is beyond the scope of this volume.

The two most likely causes are:

A   Rheumatic fever / Infective Endocarditis

In 1966 Dr Carl Bär, a Swiss dentist, presented an admirably researched treatise, which concluded that Mozart had died of infective endocarditis after frequent episodes of rheumatic fever. Severe attacks of rheumatic fever cause scarring of the heart valves, leaving them vulnerable to colonisation by blood-borne bacteria. It is these clusters of bacteria on the heart valves (vegetations), which cause infective endocarditis. The blood-borne bacteria are commonly the result of invasive clinical procedures, such as dental extractions. Mozart is known to have had dental problems in 1790-1. The "vegetations" may break off and embolise to the brain which would explain some of the symptoms of Mozart's last days.

B.   Schönlein-Henoch Purpura

Dr Peter Davies has suggested this interesting alternative diagnosis. Like Rheumatic fever Schönlein-Henoch Purpura is secondary to streptococcal infection and kidney inflammation is a feature. According to Davies, Mozart's rashes and joint pains in childhood and kidney failure in his last illness are consistent with this disease.

11   I Ballgasse 4

Beethoven

In 1809 Beethoven's brother Caspar Carl lived in an apartment on the ground floor with his wife Johanna and his son Karl, aged 3. It was his relationship with his nephew which would cause such anguish to Beethoven a few years later (see XV: 11 and XVIII: 12).

In May 1809 the French army under Napoleon Bonaparte approached Vienna for a second time.

On the first occasion in 1805 the French had marched into Vienna unopposed. This time it was decided, unwisely in the event, that the city would be defended.

Between 9pm on May 11th and 2.30pm on May 12th more than two thousand shells exploded in Vienna. Beethoven took shelter in the cellar of this house with his brother and his family, covering his head with a pillow.

Next day, with the fabric of the city in a sorry state, Vienna surrendered and Napoleon entered the Austrian capital once more.

12   I Ballgasse 6 "Zum alten Blumenstock"

Beethoven

Beethoven stayed in this inn from October 1819 until February 1820 while working on the *Missa Solemnis*. He was also involved in a bitter and protracted battle for custody of his nephew Karl (see above). Beethoven's brother had died and the composer believed that the mother of young Karl was unfit to be a parent.

Schubert

In the early nineteenth century "Zum alten Blumenstock" was a venue for the Viennese intelligentsia. In 1813 the sixteen-year-old Schubert visited the inn after watching a performance of Gluck's *Iphigenia in Tauris*. Schubert had been overwhelmed by the performance and, after a few drinks, became increasingly voluble in his praise. A university professor at a neighbouring table began to mock his youthful enthusiasm. Eyes ablaze with anger, Schubert leapt to his feet, knocking over a full tankard of beer, and a heated exchange ensued which would have ended in blows had not cooler heads intervened. This would not be the only recorded incident in which alcohol induced the normally mild-mannered Schubert to indulge in intemperate behaviour (see XV: 4).

13 I Seilerstätte 9 The Ronacher Theatre

This fine old theatre was built in 1888. In 1990 **Gottfried von Einem's** last opera *Der Tulifant* was given its première here.

Von Einem's importance in twentieth century music in Vienna was recognised when the newly-refurbished chamber music hall at the Musikverein was named after him (see XXI). He died in 1996.

14 I Seilerstätte 20 site of "Zur ungarischen Krone" inn

"The Hungarian Crown" inn stood at the corner of Seilerstätte and the Himmelpfortgasse.

Mozart

This inn was convenient for Mozart when he lived in his final residence in the Rauhensteingasse (see II: 10). In June 1791 in two letters to his wife Constanza, who was "taking the waters" in Baden, Mozart mentioned that he had lunched here, once alone and once with his pupil Süssmayer.

"The Hungarian Crown" also possessed a billiard table on which Mozart frequently played.

Billiards was a popular game in Vienna and high stakes were often involved. Mozart was passionately fond of the game and it has been suggested that his financial problems were caused in part by gambling debts incurred by betting on games of billiards, although there is no evidence to substantiate this claim.

Schubert

Schubert and his friends frequented the "Hungarian Crown"

from 1821 to 1824. A feature of the inn was a mechanical clock, which, by inserting the appropriate cylinders, played popular tunes. As early as 1822 Schubert's song *Heidenröslein* was played and later cylinders of Schubert's waltzes were also prepared.

Weber

Karl Maria von Weber stayed at the inn in 1823. Weber was in Vienna preparing for the première of *Euryanthe* at the Kärntnertor Theatre on October 25 1823.

15   I Himmelpfortgasse 17

Hugo von Hoffmansthal

In this attractive house lived Hugo von Hoffmansthal with whom Richard Strauss collaborated. Hoffmansthal supplied the libretti for *Elektra, Der Rosenkavalier, Ariadne auf Naxos, Die Frau ohne Schatten, Die Ägyptische Helene* and *Arabella*.

16   I Himmelpfortgasse 6

The café Frauenhuber was, in the eighteenth century, the elegant restaurant of Ignaz Jahn. On the first floor was a hall which seated 400 people. Concerts were held here including those of the Gesellschaft der Musikfreunde which, until it acquired its own rooms in the Tuchlauben (see IV: 10), had no permanent hall of its own.

Mozart

The commemorative plaque refers to a concert, which Mozart directed for his own benefit in November 1788. The concert featured Mozart's arrangement of the Pastorale from Handel's *Acis and Galatea* which Mozart had made for Baron von Swieten (see V: 1J).

Two other concerts are worthy of mention. On March 4th 1791 Mozart took part in a benefit concert for the clarinettist Josef Bähr, when he played his last and arguably his finest piano concerto, No. 27 in B^b (K595). His first love, Constanza's elder sister Aloysia, also took part. It was to be Mozart's last public appearance.

On January 2nd 1793, just over a year after Mozart's death, Baron von Swieten arranged the first performance of Mozart's Requiem for Constanza's benefit.

After Süssmayer had completed the Requiem, Constanza was able to give the score to Count Walsegg–Stupach, who had commissioned the work, in return for a substantial sum. However, before she handed over the score, she made an illicit copy which was used for the first performance in Jahn's rooms. Stupach found himself in an impossible position. Although he was undeniably the owner of the work, he had also claimed to be the composer (see II: 10). It was presumably embarrassment which persuaded him not to instigate litigation against Constanza.

Beethoven

The commemorative plaque also notes that, on April 6th 1797, Beethoven gave the first performance of his Quintet for Piano and Strings (Op 16). The first violin was Ignaz Schuppanzigh. The previous week Beethoven and Schuppanzigh had also performed together in Jahn's rooms a Beethoven violin sonata.

17   I Johannesgasse I

Beethoven

Beethoven moved to the fourth floor of an apartment in the house which stood on this site in November 1824. His stay here was marked by loud quarrels with his nephew Karl who was a student at the university and had fallen into bad company. In April 1825 Beethoven's landlady, frightened by the arguments and wearied by Beethoven "pounding" the piano, asked him to leave.

18   I Johannesgasse 18

Haydn

On his return from a successful (and lucrative) visit to England in 1792, Haydn lived for a short period in an apartment in the building which stood on this site. On his journey from England he had stopped at Bonn and met Beethoven who, at 21, was a viola player in the Elector's orchestra. Beethoven followed Haydn to Vienna to become his pupil, and in this house received lessons from the older master. Beethoven considered Haydn's tuition inadequate and approached Salieri and Albrechtsberger, *inter alia*, to supplement Haydn's lessons. Haydn was preoccupied with plans for a second visit to England. Even as a young man, Beethoven was suspicious of the motives of those around him, and he developed the notion that Haydn was jealous and ill-disposed towards him. This was an unwarranted aspersion; Haydn was a man without malice. Later, Beethoven would declare that he had never learnt anything from Haydn, a statement which is manifestly not true.

(It should be mentioned here that H.C. Robbins-Landon maintains that Haydn, on his return from his first visit to England, took lodgings in his old apartment at Seilerstätte 15 (see II:19 below), and not at Johannesgasse 18).

19 I Seilerstätte 15

Haydn

On this site stood the venerable "Hambergersches-Haus" which was demolished in the nineteenth century. Haydn took rooms here in 1755. He was just beginning to make his way in the world, giving lessons and playing the organ. During his stay here, he was the victim of a burglary; all his meagre possessions, including his clothes were stolen.

Beethoven

Beethoven stayed in the "Hambergersches-Haus" for about a year in 1801-2. During this period he fell in love with Countess Giulietta Guicciardi, to whom he dedicated the "Moonlight Sonata" (Op 27 No. 2). It was during this year that he realised that his hearing was becoming increasingly impaired, a fact that he carefully concealed.

20 I Seilerstätte 21

Haydn

In 1790, Haydn's patron Prince Nicolaus Esterházy died and

Haydn was released from service with a handsome pension. He took lodgings in the apartment house which stood on this site. Here he received a visit from Johann Peter Salomon of the Philharmonic Society of London who greeted Haydn with the words, "I am Salomon of London and I have come to fetch you". Haydn departed for London on December 15th 1790. On the previous evening, Mozart joined Salomon and Haydn for a farewell dinner. Salomon is believed to have offered to Mozart a similar contract to visit London in 1792, but by then Mozart was dead.

21   I Seilerstätte 30

Nicolai

The commemorative plaque records the stay in this house of Otto Nicolai. In 1841 Nicolai was engaged as conductor at the Court Opera House which was then the Kärntnertor Theatre. By careful preparation and scrupulous attention to detail, Nicolai radically raised artistic standards at the Opera, and he also played a part in the founding of a Viennese institution. Until this time there was no permanent orchestra of professional musicians for the performance of orchestral concerts. (Beethoven was obliged to hire not only the theatre but also the theatre orchestra for the performance of his symphonies). These concerts were often preceded by only one rehearsal.

On Easter Day 1842 in the Grosser Redoutensaal of the Hofburg Palace, Nicolai conducted a "Philharmonic Concert". The orchestra was that of the Court Opera. There had been several rehearsals and for the first time the Viennese heard the music of the great classical masters in well-prepared and polished performances. Thus there came into being the Vienna Philharmonic Orchestra. To this day members of this orchestra are drawn from players contracted to the State Opera (see XXI).

During his tenure at the Court Opera, Nicolai composed his best-known opera "The Merry Wives of Windsor". Having completed the opera, Nicolai approached the management of the Court Opera with a view to staging a production, but was met by endless procrastination. In high dudgeon he resigned and left Vienna in 1847.

22   I Annagasse 20

Sechter

In the house which previously stood on this site, Simon Sechter died in 1867. Though a prolific composer of ecclesiastical music and opera it is as a theorist and teacher that he is best remembered. His pupils included Schubert and Bruckner. It is a measure of the esteem in which he was held in Vienna that Schubert, just before he died in 1828, should have approached Sechter for lessons in counterpoint; this just weeks after Schubert had composed his String Quintet in C, one of the most sublime works in the chamber music repertory.

Sechter was a kindly and courteous man, and generous to a fault. It was partly due to this beneficence that he died in straitened circumstances.

23   I Annagasse 3-3a and the Annakirche

The pleasant baroque church of St. Anna, constructed by Jesuits in 1630, was an important focus of musical life in Vienna in the nineteenth century. There was a music school here which, together with the Imperial and Royal Organ School, was devoted to raising the standard of liturgical music in rural communities in Austria.

At 3-3a Annagasse there was a monastery, affiliated to the Annakirche next door, which became the "Imperial and Royal High School". The teacher training college here recruited prospective school assistants who, on graduation, were eligible for positions in elementary school.

Schubert

After leaving school at 16, Schubert enrolled at the college in the Annagasse for the 1813-14 academic year to train as a school assistant. Schubert had no vocation as a teacher, but bowed to pressure from his father who sensibly maintained that teaching was far less precarious a profession than music. For ten months, Schubert walked from the family home in Säulengasse (see XIII: 8) to the Annagasse and back six days a week. As a student, Schubert could only be described as mediocre.

Schubert's brother Ferdinand, three years his senior, also completed the teacher training course at St. Anna. In 1824 Ferdinand returned to the college as a teacher, and eventually became director of the college in 1851. Ferdinand was also a noted composer of liturgical music, and was also occasionally guilty of acts of plagiarism; he used musical material composed by his younger brother in his own works, and in at least one instance (the *Deutsches Requiem* (see XIII: 18)) he claimed a whole work by Franz Schubert as his own.

Ferdinand arranged for the first performances of two of his brother's works after the composer's death, the *Deutsche Messe* (D872) in 1846, and the beautiful and moving cantata Lazarus (which Schubert had left unfinished) in 1830. Ferdinand directed the first performances of both these works in the Annakirche.

Bruckner

In 1870 Anton Bruckner was appointed to the well-paid position of lecturer in piano, organ and theory at the teacher training college of St Anna. The following year he found himself facing a charge of sexual harassment. Bruckner had apparently made an over-familiar remark to a female student who had then lodged a formal complaint. Bruckner, absolutely mortified, asked that his teaching in future should be given only to male students. Given Bruckner's alarming propensity for falling in love with unsuitable or much younger girls, this was a wise decision.

24 I Krugerstrasse 10

Mozart

In the eighteenth century there stood here the house known as "The Blue Sabre", the home of the Russian ambassador and music-lover Prince Galitsin.

Mozart performed many times here, on the first occasion with his sister Nannerl in 1768. He also played here on five successive Thursdays in March 1784.

After Mozart's death, Constanza lived in an apartment here for a while in1795.

Haydn

In 1898 Haydn kept a small apartment here while he prepared "Creation" for performance at the Palace of Prince Schwarzenberg in the Neuer Markt (see V: 8).

Beethoven

After "The Blue Sabre" had been demolished, the imposing palace of Countess Erdödy was constructed on the site.

Countess Erdödy had an apartment on the first floor of the palace. Of Hungarian extraction, she was a fine pianist and held musical *soirées* at her home. She was estranged from her husband and lived with the knowledge of rumours that she had been involved in the murder of her son. For ten years she was on close terms with Beethoven. In the winter of 1807-8 Beethoven was her house guest, occupying a "large, desolate and lonely apartment" as described by one visitor.

In 1809 Jerome Bonaparte made an enticing offer to Beethoven. He invited Beethoven to become Kapellmeister in Kassel in Westphalia. Countess Erdödy brokered a contract with Prince Lobkowitz, Prince Kinsky and the Archduke Rudolf under which Beethoven would receive a life-long annuity on the understanding that he would remain in Austria.

25   I Krugerstrasse 13

Beethoven

After being evicted from his apartment in the Johannesgasse (see II: 17) in 1825, Beethoven moved briefly to a house which stood here. By now he was suffering from a variety of illnesses, mostly involving his digestive tract. Although virtually stone deaf he still toyed with an offer to conduct concerts in London.

26   The Hotel Bristol

Mahler

In 1897 Gustav Mahler was appointed Chief Conductor and Musical Director of the Court Opera. It was the position that Mahler had coveted most of all; to secure it he had renounced his Jewish faith and had become "a Catholic of convenience".

On arrival in Vienna he stayed at the Hotel Bristol. In the foyer he met his erstwhile employer, Bernhard Pollini, theatre director of the Hamburg Opera from which Mahler had recently resigned. Mahler must have derived considerable satisfaction from the meeting. The relationship between the two men had deteriorated and Mahler would have savoured Pollini inadvertently witnessing Mahler taking up the most prestigious post in music.

III Between St. Stephen's and the Old University

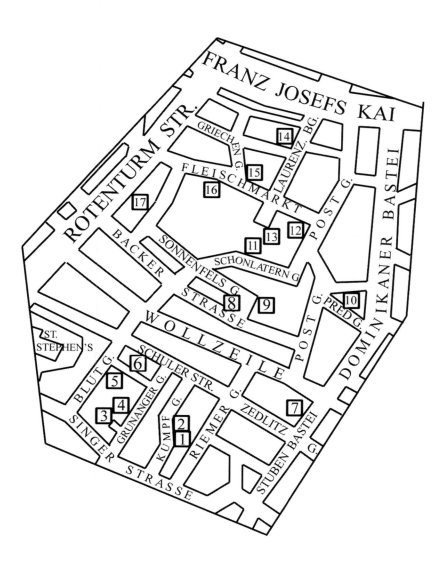

1   I Kumpfgasse 9

Wolf

Hugo Wolf lived in the "Becherlhof" in 1884. These were difficult times for Wolf; compositions were few, primarily due to depression associated with the syphilitic infection that he had contracted six years before. He spent much time trying unsuccessfully to secure performances of his music.

2   I Kumpfgasse 11

Johann Straus (father)

On this site until its demolition in 1914 stood the so-called "Ramhof". The plaque affixed to the present building marks the death here in 1849 of Johann Strauss (father). Strauss lived here with his mistress, Emilie Trampusch, a milliner 10 years his junior, from 1845 until his death.

Strauss was hardly a model of marital probity. Shortly after giving birth to her sixth and last child, Eduard, in 1835, his wife Anna discovered that her husband had recently fathered a child by his mistress Emilie. In all, Strauss and Emilie produced seven illegitimate children. When her humiliation became intolerable, Anna divorced Strauss and he moved to the house in the Kumpfgasse.

When the revolution of 1848 reached Vienna, Strauss, as K.K.Hofball-Musik Direktor, was very much an establishment figure. While his son Johann sided with the insurgents, Strauss secured his immortality with a march dedicated to a not particularly distinguished Austrian Field Marshall, Count Radetsky.

When Strauss died here from scarlet fever in 1849, all Austria mourned.

3   I Nicolaigasse

Haydn

In the Singerstrasse, backing on to this small cul-de-sac, stood the Convent of St. Nicolas where Haydn's first love, Theresa Kellner, took her vows as a nun in 1756. Having been rejected by Theresa, Haydn subsequently entered into an unhappy marriage with Theresa's elder sister Anna.

Haydn marked the induction of Theresa into the order by composing the Organ Concerto in C and the *Salve Regina* in E which he played and conducted during the ceremony. The moving Salve Regina probably reflects his own personal sadness at that time.

4   I Grünangergasse 10

Mozart

In an apartment on the first floor of this building there took place the dramatic incident which would give added ammunition to advocates of the theory that Mozart was poisoned.

The apartment was occupied by the Hofdemel family. Franz Hofdemel was a minor civil servant in the Chancery Department. He was a fellow Lodge member of Mozart and had lent money to the composer. Hofdemel's wife Maria, an attractive and vivacious woman, was a piano pupil of Mozart. The couple had a young daughter and Maria was pregnant with a second child.

The facts are not in dispute. On December 6th 1791, the day after Mozart's death, Hofdemel took a razor to his wife, inflicting severe and disfiguring lacerations to her face, neck, arms and shoulders. He then turned the razor upon himself, committing suicide by cutting his own throat. Maria survived the attack.

Rumours rapidly became rife in Vienna that Mozart had been having an affair with Maria, that her unborn child was indeed his and that Hofdemel's attack was motivated by jealous rage over his wife's alleged infidelity. Beethoven, at his most prudish, once refused to play before Maria because of the alleged relationship with Mozart.

The author Francis Carr had put forward an interesting theory; he has argued, persuasively but ultimately unconvincingly, that Hofdemel murdered Mozart by poison. His motive was either to gain revenge for the seduction of his wife, or (acting as an agent for his fellow Masons), to punish Mozart for revealing Masonic rituals in "The Magic Flute".

Schubert

This building with its low – ceilinged rooms and wooden floors was for many years the tavern called "Zum grünen Anker" (The Green Anchor). In later years, when it became an Italian restaurant, the name was retained. Recently the property has become a French restaurant and the new owners, presumably with no knowledge of musical history, have renamed the restaurant "La Créperie".

In the years 1826 and 1827 the "Green Anchor" was the haunt of Schubert and his friends. The "Anchor" is mentioned frequently in their correspondence during this period. Friends who met here included Schwind, Spaun and Schober. They tended to stay until late at night before repairing to Bogner's Café nearby. In one letter is recorded details of a large – scale snowball fight on the corner of Singerstrasse and Grüngangergasse involving the Schubert circle. In 1827 the "Anchor" , for whatever reason, fell out of favour with the group.

5   I Domgasse 4

Georg Hellmesberger

In this house from 1850 lived the distinguished violinist, conductor and professor at the Vienna Conservatory, Georg Hellmesberger.

In view of his subsequent achievements it is interesting to note a report in the archives of the " Stadtkonvict". (He was for a time a fellow chorister of Schubert in the court choir): "Hellmesberger to be given an emphatic rebuke in the name of the Lord High Steward's Office for insufficient application to his studies".

6   I Schulerstrasse 8   (Domgasse 5)

Mozart

On the first floor of this modest but attractive seventeenth century house is the apartment that Mozart occupied for the 2½ years which marked the zenith of his career in Vienna. The façade of the Schulerstrasse aspect has remained virtually unchanged since Mozart's time. The only significant modification is that, during the nineteenth century, the doorway was bricked up and entrance is now gained by way of the Domgasse.

Mozart's apartment comprised four large and two small rooms, together with the kitchen and small utility rooms. Of the two rooms with their familiar bay windows overlooking the Schulerstrasse, the larger was the family sitting room, and the smaller was, in all probability, Mozart's study. This room features richly decorated stucco, the work of a former owner, Albert Camesina (the "Imperial Stucco Worker"), no doubt as a showcase for his craftsmanship.

Some of the rooms were acquired by the City of Vienna in 1941, and became a small museum. The remaining rooms were purchased in 1976 and the apartment restored to its former state. Coins found between the floor-boards, dating from the late eighteenth century, confirm that the present floor is the one upon which Mozart trod. Today the apartment, the most substantial to be occupied by Mozart, is a shrine for music lovers the world over. Mozart, Constanza and their son Karl (born during the previous week), moved here in September 1784. The four-fold increase in rent compared to his previous lodgings at the "Trattnerhof" (see IV: 1) are an indication of his burgeoning confidence in his future and his increased income at this time.

In December 1784, Mozart became a Freemason; Masonry continued to be important to him for the rest of his life. (see IV: 13).

In January 1785 he received a courtesy call from Josef Haydn. Together with two composer friends, Vanhal and Dittersdorf, they played some of the six string quartets that Mozart had composed recently.

In February 1785 his father Leopold arrived for a ten-week stay. Haydn paid another visit, and it was the proudest moment of

Leopold's life when Haydn took him to one side and informed him that Wolfgang was the greatest composer he knew.

Leopold was present at the "Mehlgrube" (see V : 10) for the first of six subscription concerts, for each of which Mozart composed a new piano concerto. This first concert included the D minor concerto (K466). These concerts were heavily subscribed and enthusiastically received.

Early in 1786, a 7-year old prodigy from Pressburg, Johann Nepomuk Hummel, came to stay with Mozart as his (non-paying) pupil.

Also at the beginning of 1786, Mozart composed a one-act opera *Der Schauspieldirector* at the command of the Emperor Josef II for performance at the Orangery at the Schönbrunn Palace. (see XVI ; 3B).

His most substantial work of this year was "The Marriage of Figaro", which received its première on May 1st 1786.

There was sadness in November of that year when the Mozarts' 3-week-old son Johann died.

Suddenly, the tide turned for Mozart. He fell out of favour with the Viennese, and the names on his subscription list dwindled to one: that of Baron von Swieten (see V: 1J). He was obliged to leave this expensive apartment and find a succession of cheaper lodgings, none of which have survived to this day.

Beethoven

In April 1789, the 17-year-old Beethoven travelled to Vienna from his home in Bonn, to seek lessons from Mozart. The story (perhaps apocryphal) goes that Mozart, having listened to Beethoven improvising, turned to friends in an adjoining room and advised them to watch out for Beethoven, one day he would give the world something to talk about. Beethoven may have been given a few casual lessons from Mozart, but then received news from Bonn of the serious illness of his mother, and was obliged to return home.

It is of interest to note the opinion of Beethoven with regard to Mozart's piano technique: "Too choppy, no legato". This somewhat disparaging judgement is understandable when it is remembered that Mozart was brought up with the harpsichord. It would be surprising if the style of Mozart's playing was not one of the clipped precision demanded by that instrument.

Only at the end of the eighteenth century were larger and more powerful pianos produced which enabled Beethoven to take the art of piano playing to a new dimension.

Brahms

In September 1862, the 29-year-old Johannes Brahms visited Vienna for the first time. He paid an early call on Professor Julius Epstein, pianist and teacher at the Conservatoire, who lived in Mozart's old apartment. Here, with the string quartet of Josef Helmesberger, they played over the two new piano quartets of Brahms (in G minor and A major). Helmesberger was enraptured, declaring Brahms to be Beethoven's heir.

| 7 | I Stubenbastei 14 |

Schubert

Between autumn 1823 and spring 1824 Schubert lived in an apartment on the first-floor of the house which stood on this site as a guest of Josef Huber, a member of the Schubert circle. Tall and pedantic, Huber was also a man of immense kindness, taking in Schubert at a time when the composer was both penniless and also ravaged by venereal disease. Schubert was in the throes of the secondary stage of syphilis. The characteristic rash was present together with nausea and alopecia.

As the symptoms subsided, Schubert turned his attention to the two works with which he was preoccupied ; the song cycle *Die Schöne Müllerin* and the incidental music to the play *Rosamunde*.

Schubert took to wearing a wig until his natural hair returned.

| 8 | I Dr Ignaz Seipel Platz |

The Great Hall of the Old University. (Aula)

Haydn

On March 27th, 1808, a gala performance of Haydn's oratorio "Creation" was given at the Old Hall of the University to celebrate the composer's seventy-sixth birthday. Although he was old and very weak, Haydn signified his wish to be present. A carriage provided by Princess Esterházy brought him from his home to the hall where he was greeted by a large crowd of well-wishers in the square outside. He was borne into the hall in a sedan chair to an accompaniment of trumpets and drums and seated in the place of honour alongside Prince Esterházy, his former employer. All the great and good of Vienna were present for the performance which was conducted by Antonio Salieri. At the interval Haydn was overcome by emotion and it was deemed wise that he should be taken home. As he prepared to leave, Beethoven stepped forward to kiss the hand of his former teacher. Haydn died 9 months later.

Beethoven

On December 8th 1813, a charity concert was given in the Old Hall in aid of wounded Austrian soldiers. The opening work was the first performance of Beethoven's Symphony No. 7 in A, which was rapturously received.

The last work in the concert was a novelty. At the behest of Johann Mälzel, the inventor of the metronome, Beethoven composed a work featuring Mälzel's latest invention, the " Panharmonicon", an instrument powered by bellows which imitated the instruments of a military band. This work, "The Battle of Vittoria", celebrated the recent victory by Wellington over Napoleon in the Peninsular War. Playing in the orchestra were such distinguished musicians as Salieri, Meyerbeer, Hummel and Spohr. Beethoven conducted, although his hearing by then was so severely impaired that he lost control, and the performance was rescued by the conductor Michael Umlauf, standing beside Beethoven.

Bruckner

In 1875 Anton Bruckner took a lectureship in harmony and counterpoint at the University despite the vigorous opposition of Eduard Hanslick, the respected but much-feared critic. Hanslick held the position of Professor of History and Aesthetics of Music. Hanslick was a gifted and articulate writer on music, but with severe limitations. Programme music was anathema to him and he became a devotee of Brahms, who he felt was the true successor to Beethoven in advancing the cause of "pure" music. He developed a poisonous antipathy to the music of Wagner, and it was Hanslick's bigoted articles on the music of Wagner and his admirers (particularly Bruckner) which prolonged the acrimonious dispute between the followers of Wagner and Brahms for so long.

Hanslick enlisted Brahms's services as a pianist for his lecture on Beethoven. Brahms, whose pianistic technique was formidable, played Beethoven's great Sonata in C minor, Op 111.

9   Dr Ignaz Seipel Platz

Stadtkonvict (The Imperial Boarding School)

Schubert

In August 1808, Schubert's father responded to an advertisement in a Viennese newspaper which advised that there were vacancies pending in the Imperial Court chapel choir. The following month Schubert's father duly presented his 11-year-old son at the Stadtkonvict for the audition. His examiners included the Director, Dr Innocenz Lang, and the Hofkapellmeister, Antonio Salieri. Schubert was awarded one of the two places on offer and became part of that 500-year-old tradition which eventually became the Vienna Boys Choir. As an Imperial Chorister, Schubert was automatically enrolled at the Stadtkonvict, receiving lessons at the Gymnasium next door and thus benefited from the best education available to commoners in Vienna.

The building was as spartan within as it was forbidding from the external aspect. Heating was inadequate, the food sparse and of poor quality and discipline was strictly enforced by means of birching. The work-load was unrelenting; academic lessons during the day were followed by music lessons in the evening, and in addition there were frequent rehearsals and performances in the Imperial Chapel at the Hofburg (see: 1F). The only holiday allowed was a brief one in the autumn.

Notwithstanding these privations, the five years that Schubert spent at the Stadkonvict were essentially happy and fulfilling. He took particular pleasure in playing the violin in the school orchestra. This orchestra had been founded by Josef von Spaun, a law student, who was eight years older than Schubert. Spaun became the first and most steadfast of the group of friends which would enrich Schubert's life in the years to come.

The orchestra was conducted by the Principal Music Tutor Wenzel Ruzicka, who would in due course allow Schubert to take charge on occasions. The orchestra was of a reasonable standard. It became fashionable for the Viennese, on pleasant summer evenings, to carry chairs to the University Square and listen to the concerts through the open windows. The repertoire of the orchestra included the symphonies of Haydn and Mozart, and the first two of Beethoven.

Schubert's promise was recognised at an early stage; Ruzicka famously declared of Schubert: "this one has learnt it from God". Salieri was sufficiently impressed by Schubert's precocious talent to invite him to twice-weekly private lessons at his home.

There were other diversions; in 1809 during the French bombardment, a howitzer shell crashed through the roof of the Stadtkonvict before exploding in the room of a teacher, Josef Walch, who was fortunately absent at the time. Walch, a most unpopular teacher, would later fail Schubert at mathematics.

In 1812 Schubert's voice broke, an event which he recorded in the alto part of the score of a Mass by Peter Winter: "Franz Schubert crowed for the last time, 26th July 1812".

Exempted from choir duties, Schubert devoted all his time to composition, to the detriment of other subjects in which his work fell below the required standard. Sensing that it was time to leave, Schubert enrolled in the teacher training college of St Anna (see II: 23).

He dedicated his Symphony No. 1 in D to the Director of Stadtkonvict, Dr Lang.

10   I Postgasse 6

Brahms

Brahms moved to an apartment on the fourth floor of this house in November 1866, living there until the end of 1867. During this time he was much preoccupied with preparing for the first performance of his newly-composed *Ein Deutsches Requiem*. (The fifth movement with its beautiful soprano solo would be added later).

It had been Brahms's life-long ambition to become Director of the Philharmonic Society in Hamburg, his home city. During this year the post became vacant. Brahms was deeply embittered when he was passed over for the position (for the second time), and decided that Vienna would become his permanent home.

11   I Schönlaterngasse 7a

Schumann

The plaque affixed to this building records the stay here of Robert Schumann between September 1838 and March 1839. At home in Leipzig, Schumann was the editor of a musical newspaper, the *Neue Zeitschrift*, founded with the avowed intention of raising the standard of musical journalism, with intelligent commentary on the rapidly-changing face of nineteenth century music, and raising the status of performers.

Schumann was deeply in love with the gifted young pianist Clara Wieck who, although not yet nineteen, was already establishing an enviable reputation throughout Europe. The relationship between Schumann and Clara was opposed with implacable hostility by Clara's father who considered Schumann an unsuitable suitor for his daughter on both social and financial grounds. He would not countenance any talk of marriage until Schumann's social status and financial situation had improved considerably.

Schumann therefore came to Vienna both to increase his own standing as a composer and to move the *Neue Zeitschrift* to the Austrian capital. In both he was unsuccessful. He found journalism in Vienna in the grip of the official Censor, in which it would remain until the revolution of 1848. His attempts to seek a licence for his journal were met by bureaucratic obduracy which proved insurmountable.

He did produce some compositions for the piano, including *Arabesque* Op18, *Humoresque* Op20 and *Faschingsschwank Aus Wien* Op26, but Vienna showed little interest.

There was one noteworthy event; Schumann paid a courtesy call on Schubert's brother Ferdinand in the Kettenbrückengasse (see IX:14). Schubert had by then been dead for ten years. In a pile of priceless manuscripts Schumann discovered, to his joy and amazement, the scores of operas, four masses and five symphonies, including Schubert's last, No. 9 in C major (The Great).

12 I Fleischmarkt 28

Mozart

On October 6th 1762 the six-year-old Mozart, together with his parents and his sister arrived in Vienna for his first visit. The Mozarts had travelled to the Austrian capital by the mail-boat down the River Danube. They stayed for their first night in Vienna, and perhaps a few nights, at an inn which stood on this site, 'The White Ox'.

13 I Fleischmarkt 24

Kammeroper

The Kammeroper (Vienna Chamber Opera) offers performances of early and small-scale chamber operas twice-weekly. (In summer it moves to the Schlosstheater at Schönbrunn (see XVI : 3C)). The theatre has a capacity of 300.

14 I Laurenzerberg 5

Von Suppé

Franz Von Suppé lived in an apartment house which stood on this site from autumn 1883 to November 1887. By now his career was in decline, eclipsed by the phenomenal success of Johann Strauss (son).

15 I Fleischmarkt 11

Griechenbeisl

This ancient inn with its numerous small vaulted rooms has been a tavern since the fifteenth century. Famous guests have left their signatures on the ceiling of the "Mark Twain Room", (Twain being one of those who left their autograph here).

The signatures of Mozart, Beethoven, Schubert, Wagner and Brahms are regarded as authentic.

16 I Fleischmarkt 14

Fux

In the house that stood on this site Johann Josef Fux died in 1741.

Herbeck

A commemorative plaque high on the ornate façade records the birth here of Johann Ritter von Herbeck in 1831, Herbeck was one of the most influential musicians of the nineteenth century. There were compositions by him, but it is as a conductor that he is best remembered. He had his finger in all the important musical pies of Vienna. He was at some time conductor of the concerts of the Gesellschaft der Musikfreunde (where he preceded and succeeded Brahms), he was Director of the Court Opera and also conducted the best choir in Vienna, the "Singverein".

Herbeck was well-versed in the intrigues and political manoeuvring which were such a feature of public life in Vienna

Herbeck, together with Brahms and the critic Eduard Hanslick (see III : 8), was an adjudicator appointed by the Austrian government to award an annual scholarship to assist "young, talented but impoverished artists". In 1875 the panel presented the award to a hitherto unknown Czech composer. Within two years the awardee,

Antonin Dvořák, would achieve world-wide fame.

It was Herbeck's patience and diplomacy which persuaded Schubert's friend Anselm Hüttenbrenner to relinquish the score of the "Unfinished Symphony" (see V : 13). Herbeck conducted the first performance of the work at a memorable concert in 1865 in the large room of the Redoutensäle (see V : 1G).

17   I Rotenturmstrasse 12

Lindenkeller

Claimed to be Vienna's oldest restaurant, dating from 1435, the Lindenkeller boasted Brahms amongst its regular clientèle.

IV Between St. Stephen's and the Freyung

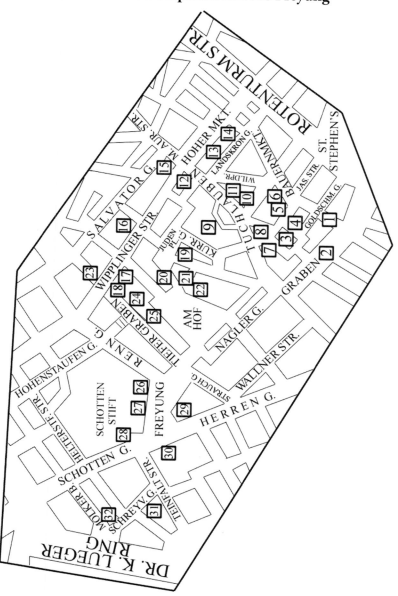

Trattnerhof

Mozart

Until its demolition in 1911 there stood here one of the best-known and most prestigious apartment houses in Vienna. The upper floors comprised apartments for over 600 people and the ground floor was let to commercial enterprises.

Mozart and his wife Constanza moved into an apartment on the third floor in January 1784. They were in the second year of their marriage.

The building, constructed in 1776, was owned by Johann von Trattner, an extremely wealthy publisher, printer and bookseller. His wife, 40 years his junior, was a piano pupil of Mozart.

Although his apartment was small, the building suited Mozart very well. It included the deconsecrated St George's chapel, which Mozart was able to use as a concert hall. On three successive Wednesdays in March 1784 Mozart gave three highly successful subscription concerts here, for each of which he composed a new piano concerto:- No. 14 in E^b (K449), No. 15 in B^b (K450) and No. 16 in D (K451). His subscription list contained 172 names, which meant that the hall was full to overflowing.

In May 1784 Mozart purchased a pet starling, which, to his delight, was able to sing a passably accurate version of the finale of his newly-composed Piano Concerto No. 17 in G (K453).

On September 21st 1784, Constanza gave birth to a son, Karl Thomas, one of only two of her children to survive infancy.

After Mozart's death, Constanza strongly discouraged Karl from making a career in music. (She had ambitions for her younger son Wolfgang junior but he never rose above mediocrity (see I)). Karl eventually became a civil servant in Italy. He died in 1858 at the age of 74 and is buried just outside Milan. Like his brother he never married.

In September 1784 the Mozarts moved to the Schulerstrasse (see III: 10).

2 I Graben

Pestsäule

The Pestsäule (Plague column), completed in 1693, is the most familiar feature of the Graben. This baroque sculpture was commissioned by Emperor Leopold I to celebrate deliverance from the Great Plague of 1679.

The Graben and the Kärntnerstrasse, both now pedestrianised, are disappointing for the historian. The Kärntnerstrasse was widened in the late nineteenth century and, in consequence, many buildings were sacrificed. The mundane architecture of the Graben and the Kärntnerstrasse is uninspiring and with little historical interest. The Pestsäule remains and would have been a familiar landmark to Haydn, Mozart, Beethoven and later composers.

3 St. Peter's Church

The Baroque Peterskirche was completed in 1733

Mozart

Two of Mozart's children were baptised in this church: Karl in September 1784 (see above) and a short-lived daughter, Theresia, in December 1787.

When Mozart was on his death-bed in December 1791 (see III: 10), his sister-in-law Sophie came to St. Peter's to ask for a priest to attend him. At first her request was refused and only after desperate pleading by the distraught Sophie would one of "those clerical brutes" (her description) agree to visit the dying composer.

4 I Goldschmiedgrasse 6

"Zum goldenen Rebhuhn" (The Golden Partridge)

The building was demolished in 1879. (The present Café Rebhuhn is today located next door at Goldschmiedgasse 8). In

---

this coffee-house Josef Lanner formed a group of five musicians, including Johann Strauss (father), to play music for dancing. Schubert and his friends were frequently present.

In 1828, after an altercation with the landlord of another tavern, the Rebhuhn with its dense smoky atmosphere became a regular haunt of the Schubert circle.

5   I Petersplatz 11

Beethoven

The present building occupies the site of two adjoining apartment houses in which Beethoven lived at the turn of the nineteenth century.

Between May and December 1799 he lived in an apartment on the third floor of the building which stood on the corner of the Goldsmiedgasse. This was the period in which the Piano Sonata Op 13 (the *Pathétique*) and the String Quartet Op 18 were composed. Among the pupils who laboriously climbed the winding stairs to his rooms was Countess Therese von Brunswick who has been mooted as a possible intended recipient of the letter, which Beethoven wrote to "the immortal beloved" (see VII: 6).

During the winter 1802-3 Beethoven lived in an apartment in the house next door, known as "Zum silbernen Vogel", on the corner of the Freisingergasse. Beethoven was coming to terms with the devastating realisation that he was becoming deaf. His anguish had been committed to paper the previous summer in the so-called "Heiligenstadt Testament" (see XV: 8).

6   I Bauernmarkt 4/ Brandstätte 5

Gundelhof

Schubert

In the early nineteenth century the Gundelhof was the best-known musical salon in Vienna. It was the home of the remarkable Sonnleithner family. Ignaz von Sonnleithner was a lawyer and professor of commercial science. He had a splendid bass voice and had been on friendly terms with Mozart, Haydn, Beethoven and Salieri. His brother Josef was secretary of the Hoftheater. It was Josef who suggested to Beethoven the subject for the opera, which became Fidelio, and also furnished the libretto for the first (1805) version. It was a translation of Bouilly's *Léonore, ou l'amour conjugal.* Ignaz's son Leopold was a contemporary of Schubert at the Stadtkonvict(see III: 9). Leopold strove ceaselessly to promote Schubert's music.

The Sonnleithners were co-founders of the Gesellschaft der Musikfreunde, which remains today Vienna's most prestigious music society. The early meetings of the Society took place in the elegant and spacious drawing room of the Gundelhof, which could comfortably seat 120. These meetings were held every Friday evening during the summer months and fortnightly during winter. It was Leopold who introduced Schubert into this cultured intellectual milieu.

Among the works of Schubert, which were first brought to public notice here were the songs *Erlkönig, Gretchen am Spinnrad* and *Das Dörfchen.*

The Gundelhof was demolished in 1877.

7   I Milchgasse 1 / Petersplatz

Mozart

The commemorative plaque on the Milchgasse aspect stating that "Mozart lived here in 1781 and composed *Entführung aus dem Serail*" is misleading. The plaque was previously affixed to the building, which preceded the present edifice, the so-called "Eye of God" house.

In May 1781 Mozart was obliged to leave his lodgings at the Deutschordenshaus (see II: 2) at a moment's notice, and hurriedly found new accommodation with a widow, Frau Cäcilie Weber on the second floor of the house on Petersplatz. Mozart's original intention was to stay for only one week before returning to Salzburg, but was overtaken by the dramatic events at the Deutschordenshaus (see III: 6).

When news of the move reached Leopold Mozart in Salzburg he was appalled. He recalled only too clearly his son's infatuation with the Weber's daughter Aloysia only three years before. Although Aloysia was now married and had left home, there were still three unmarried daughters in the apartment at the "Eye of God" house. When rumours reached Leopold of the developing relationship between Wolfgang and Aloysia's younger sister Constanza, Leopold's worst fears were realised; his distrust of the Weber family was absolute.

Mozart's letter to his father denying the relationship hardly allayed Leopold's anxiety. "I work in the mornings (presumably on the first act of *Entführung*) and only 'fool around' with Constanza in the evenings".

After four months, with the tongues of the gossips wagging in earnest, Mozart deemed it wise to leave the Weber apartment and find lodgings nearby in the Graben. (see V: 18). The lockplate from the door of Mozart's apartment is to be found in the Mozart museum on the Schulerstrasse.

8   I Tuchlauben 8

Berg

A commemorative plaque marks the site of the building in which Alban Berg was born in 1885. His father owned a bookshop on the corner of Milchgasse and Kühfussgasse.

9   Kleebattgasse/Kurrentgasse

Haslinger's publishing house

This long-established business was formerly Steiner & Co. In 1826 Steiner's partner Tobias Haslinger took over the business. Schubert offered his works to Haslinger after the former lost faith in Anton Diabelli. Schubert was convinced that Diabelli was cheating him.

In 1823 Schubert met Weber in Steiner's shop shortly after the première at the Theater an der Wien (see X: 4) of *Euryanthe*. When

Schubert commented to Weber that he had preferred *Der Freischütz*
Weber took umbrage and the friendship rapidly cooled.

Among Schubert's works published by Haslinger was the song-
cycle *Winterreise.*

10 I Tuchlauben 12 – 14

Gesellschaft der Musikfreunde

Although founded in 1812 the Society did not acquire its own
rooms until 1822 when it rented the building at Tuchlauben 12
known as "Zum roten Igel" (The Red Hedgehog). In 1829 the
Society purchased the building, demolished it and constructed
Vienna's first purpose–built concert hall on the site (seating 700)
together with a conservatory and archives. The Society moved into
its present building on the Karlsplatz (see XXI) in 1870, after which
the buildings on the Tuchlauben were demolished.

Schubert

Shortly before his death in 1828 Schubert gave the only concert
in his short life that was devoted solely to his own music. This
concert at the "Red Hedgehog" included his Piano Trio in Eb
(D929). Although acclaimed by the audience, the concert did not
receive a single mention in the Viennese press; the event had been
overshadowed by the arrival of Paganini.

Next door to the "Red Hedgehog" at Tuchlauben 14 stood the
"Blue Hedgehog" ("Zum blauen Igel"). Schubert lived here as a guest
of Franz Schober and his mother. Schubert was allocated two rooms
and a music room on the second floor. He lived here from March
1827 until August 1828 when he moved to his brother Ferdinands's
house in Wieden (see IX: 14).

Brahms

The "Red Hedgehog" included a restaurant of the same name,
which became a favourite haunt of Brahms. In 1889 supporters of
Brahms and Bruckner arranged a dinner here for the two composers
to try to dispel the ill-feeling between them. This ill-will stemmed

from Brahms's description of Bruckner's symphonies as "symphonic boa constrictors". Both men preferred simple fare and enjoyed their meal of smoked ham and dumplings, but no rapport developed between them.

Brahms made his Viennese début at the Gesellschaft in 1862 with a programme which included his Piano Quartet in G minor.

11   I Tuchlauben 20 /Landskrongasse 5

Schubert

In the early nineteenth century the house which stood on this site, known as "Zum Winter", was the home of Franz von Schober and his wealthy mother and younger sister.

In the autumn of 1816 Schober persuaded Schubert to give up the profession of teaching, leave his parental home and live in the Schober household. The plan was for Schubert to devote himself entirely to composition and pay rent when he could from fees earned from publishers.

Many of Schubert's biographers (and some of his friends) have blamed Schober for leading Schubert down the path of licentiousness which culminated in Schubert contracting syphilis in 1823. Schober was something of a dilettante; an amoral self-indulgent hedonist. He dabbled in poetry, painting, printing and was also at one time secretary to Franz Liszt.

Schober was also good company; a witty conversationalist with a brilliant mind. He was very supportive to Schubert, offering lodgings and financial help.

In March 1817 Schober persuaded the distinguished but ageing operatic baritone Johann Michael Vogl to visit the house in order to make the acquaintance of Schubert and his music. Sceptical at first, Vogl soon recognised the stature of the songs, and through Vogl's enthusiastic advocacy these songs were soon well-known in the musical salons of Vienna.

Among the songs composed here were *"Ganymed"*, *"An die Musik"*, (with words by Schober) and *"Der Tod und das Mädchen"* ("Death and the Maiden").

12   I Tuchlauben 27

Mozart

Mozart moved into an apartment of the house which stood on the corner of Schultergasse in December 1787. His career as a free-lance composer was now in decline and it must have been a relief when he was appointed Kammermusikus (Imperial and Royal Chamber Composer) in succession to the recently deceased Gluck, albeit at a salary less than half that of his predecessor. His duty was to compose minuets and German dances for the masked balls held in the large and small Redoutensäle at the Hofburg Palace.

Mozart once endorsed a receipt for his salary with the wry and telling remark: "Too much for what I do, too little for what I could do".

The only substantial composition written during the seven months that he lived here is his penultimate piano concerto, the rather disappointing "Coronation Concerto", No. 26 in D (K537).

On December 27th 1787 the Mozarts' fourth child, a short-lived daughter named Theresia, was born here.

13   I Landskrongasse 4-6

Mozart

This is the approximate site of the Masonic lodge, the "Benefice", which Mozart joined in December 1784. It was subsequently amalgamated with two other lodges to form the "New-crowned Hope" Lodge.

Although Mozart's motives for becoming a Freemason may have been primarily to promote his career by the cultivation of brother masons as potential patrons, there can be no doubt that Masonry became very important to him. Mozart was a man of the Enlightenment in which the primacy of church and state was brought into question. He was stimulated by the company of like-minded free-thinking men and it may be that Mozart considered that the Masonic movement represented the spirit of the Enlightenment.

Mozart composed a number of works for the Masons, the best-known being the "Masonic Funeral Music" (K477).

14 **I Hohermarkt I**

Mozart

The building which stood here in the eighteenth century was owned by Count Walsegg-Stuppach, who commissioned the Requiem from Mozart in rather strange circumstances. (See II:10). Mozart's brother Mason Michael Puchberg had an apartment here and also ran his textile business from an office in this building. Puchberg is assured of immortality for having come to the financial rescue of Mozart on so many occasions.

From a letter written by Mozart to his wife from Dresden addressed to this house, it may be deduced that Puchberg's kindness also extended to offering hospitality to Constanza while her husband was away.

15 **I Wipplingerstrasse 2**

Schubert

An undistinguished modern office block occupies the site of a house in which Schubert shared one room on the third floor with his friend Johann Mayerhofer from the end of 1818 until Schubert departed in 1820. On the ground floor was a tobacconist's emporium, which was convenient as both men were addicted to their pipes.

They lived a Bohemian existence; Mayerhofer wrote poetry and Schubert composed. There was hardly any money and the single dark room contained only a decrepit piano and some old furniture.

Mayerhofer was a law student. He was intelligent, of kindly disposition and an idealist. He also suffered episodes of severe clinical depression, which would lead to him taking his own life in 1836.

Schubert's setting of Mayerhofer's poem *Erlafsee* was the first work of his to be published. Notwithstanding his poverty-stricken existence, Schubert was very happy during the time that he lived here with Mayerhofer.

Among the works composed here were the "Trout quintet" (D667) and the remarkable "Quartetsatz", the unfinished D703.

His operas *Die Zwillingsbrüder* and *Zauberharfe* were also conceived here.

16 I Wipplingerstrasse 14

Mozart

Mozart and his wife Constanza moved into an apartment on the third-floor of the house that stood here, "The Little Herberstein House" in December 1782. The apartment comprised a small ante-room, a kitchen, bedroom and a long narrow living room. In January Mozart organised a private ball here, utilising an adjacent empty apartment placed at his disposal by his landlord Baron Wetzlar von Plankenstern. The ball lasted from six o'clock in the evening until seven o'clock the following morning.

In this apartment Mozart met his finest librettist Lorenzo da Ponte.

Mozart lived here for three months. His landlord declined to charge him any rent.

17 I Wipplingerstrasse 19 (corner of Färbergasse)

Mozart

On this site stood the house known as the "Red Sword" in which Mozart resided in 1768 and again in 1782.

In 1768, at the age of 12, he stayed here with his family while composing his opera *La Finta Semplice* which his father had persuaded Emperor Josef II to sanction. To Leopold's fury, intrigue and procrastinations delayed production of the opera indefinitely and it was not performed in Vienna.

He also composed his singspiel *Bastien und Bastienne* here which received its first performance in the garden of Dr Mesner (see VII: 4).

In July 1782 Mozart, now 26, moved into the house in

preparation for his marriage to Constanza Weber. The young couple lived here until December 1782 when they moved the short distance to Wipplingerstrasse 14 (see IV: 16).

18 I Wipplingerstrasse 21 (corner of Tiefer Graben)

Mozart

This is the site of the former monastery of St Cajetan, built by the order of Theatines. In August 1773, the seventeen-year old Mozart, together with his father, visited the monastery and performed a violin concerto in the chapel.

The monastery was abolished by order of Emperor Josef II in 1783.

Schubert

After abolition the monastery became an apartment building, which has also since been demolished.

In 1821 Schubert rented a room here alone, having left the apartment he shared with Mayerhofer in the same street (see IV: 15). A new member of the Schubert circle, the artist Moritz von Schmind, made a pen-and-ink drawing of part of the room showing a rather ancient forte-piano and an untidy pile of manuscripts.

This period of living alone did not appear to suit Schubert. He missed the company and intellectual stimulation of Mayerhofer and found the daily routine of fending for himself irksome.

19 I Judenplatz 3 and 4

Mozart

In 1895 the two houses associated with Mozart were replaced by a single building. Although Mozart's homes no longer exist, the quiet ambiance of the pedestrianised Judenplatz must be very much as it was in Mozart's time. The commemorative plaque makes reference only to Mozart's stay at No. 3 in 1783.

Judenplatz 3 (corner of Kurrentgasse)

Mozart and his wife Constanza moved to a first floor apartment here in April 1783 and stayed here for seven months. They had married the previous August.

On June 17th their first child Raimund Leopold was born. According to Constanza's own account (to Vincent and Mary Novello) Mozart was working on his String Quartet in D Minor (K421) while his wife was in labour and incorporated her cries into the work. (Wolfgang Hildesheimer has suggested that the unexpected forte passage in the andante, with two octave leaps followed by a minor tenth, represents Constanza *in extremis*.)

In July the Mozarts travelled to Salzburg to introduce Constanza to Mozart's father and sister, leaving their baby with a nurse in the Neubau district (see XI: 9).

The Mozarts must have anticipated their visit to Salzburg with some apprehension; Constanza was well aware of her father-in-law's hostility towards her and Mozart, in a letter to his father, confessed that he was fearful of arrest by his former employer, the Archbishop of Salzburg.

During their stay in Salzburg their child died. Among the other works completed here were the Horn Concertos Nos. 2 and 3 (K417 and K447). In January 1784 the Mozarts moved to the Trattnerhof in the Graben (see III:1).

Judenplatz 4

Early in 1789 the Mozarts moved to this house, which was known as "Zur Mutter Gottes" ("To the Mother of God"). They would remain here until September 1790. By now Mozart was tasting the bitterness of failure and disillusionment and his productivity declined, although the virtuosity of his clarinettist friend Anton Stadler inspired him to compose his sublime Clarinet Quintet (K581).

Constanza became ill and was advised by her physician to visit the expensive spa town of Baden for a "cure". Once again Mozart turned to Michael Puchberg for financial assistance.

In November 1789 the Mozart's fifth child Anna Maria was born here but died within the hour.

Mozart received a commission for a new Italian opera, *Così fan Tutte*, and collaborated for the last time with Lorenzo da Ponte. On New Year's Eve 1790 Mozart held a "small opera rehearsal" here to which he invited Puchberg and Haydn.

At the end of September 1790 Constanza and her one surviving child Karl moved to the Mozarts final residence in the Rauhensteingasse (see II:10). (Mozart was away in Frankfurt).

20   Ledererhof

In the Ledererhof was the apartment of Josef Karl Rosenbaum who was secretary to Prince Esterházy and friend of Joseph Haydn who was also for many years in the employ of the Prince. Rosenbaum was a prime mover in one of the more curious and bizarre episodes in Viennese musical history.

Rosenbaum subscribed to the theories of Professor Franz Gall of the University of Vienna. Gall postulated the theory that the brain of a genius was different from that of ordinary mortals and, further, that these differences were reflected in the anatomy of the inside of the skull and were measurable. Clearly, unless the genius in question was remarkably co-operative, he had to be dead before examination could take place. Thus in early nineteenth century Vienna there arose the strange and morbid fascination in acquiring and studying the skulls of the geniuses of the day.

Haydn died in 1809. Shortly after his burial in what is today the Haydn Park (see XVII: 14) Rosenbaum and an accomplice bribed a gravedigger to open Haydn's grave and remove the head. The theft was discovered in 1820 when Prince Esterházy ordered the exhumation of Haydn's remains in preparation for re-interment in a tomb of honour at Eisenstadt.

Rosenbaum's behaviour throughout this episode was reprehensible. When the Prince offered a reward for the return of the skull, Rosenbaum submitted a skull, purported to be that of Haydn, but which in fact was that of a young man.

Many years after Rosenbaum's death, Haydn's skull came into the possession of the Gesellschaft der Musikfreunde. The society ignored all entreaties to release the relic until 1954 when, at last, Haydn's skull was reunited with the remainder of the skeleton in the tomb at Eisenstadt.

Rosenbaum, married to the opera singer Theresa Gassmann, was an inveterate theatre-goer and a meticulous if acerbic diarist. He evidently had little time for the music of Schubert as the following entries illustrate:-

On Schubert's opera *Die Zwillingsbrüder*:

"Nothing to recommend it; Schubert's friends made a great deal of noise, others hissed.

On *Die Zauberharfe*:

"Wretched trash".

On *Rosamunde*:

"Empty, tedious, unnatural".

Rosenbaum was present at most of the major musical events in Vienna in his time, (including the première of Beethoven's "Choral Symphony") and his observations give an evocative insight into these great occasions.

21 | I Collalto Palace, Am Hof

Mozart

On October 9th 1762 Leopold Mozart took his six-year-old son Wolfgang and his daughter Nannerl to the Collalto Palace where the children performed on the harpsichord. It marked Mozart's debut in the Austrian capital. (The Collalto family still maintains an apartment here).

Such was the success of the concert that Leopold was inundated by invitations from the Viennese nobility, including an Imperial summons from Schonbrünn Palace to perform before Empress Maria Theresa (see XVI: (3)A).

22 | Jesuit Church, Am Hof

This church stands next to the Collalto Palace.

Mozart

In 1773 the 17-year-old Mozart visited Vienna with his father in a vain attempt to secure an appointment at the Imperial Court. During his visit, on August 8th 1773, Leopold Mozart conducted a performance of his son's "Dominican Mass" (K66) in the church Am Hof.

In June 1783 Mozart's fifth child Anna Maria was born, but died within the hour. Clergy from Am Hof were summoned to perform an emergency baptism.

Bruckner

In one of the many disappointments of his early days in Vienna, Bruckner was unsuccessful in January 1877 when he applied for the post of conductor at the church Am Hof.

23 Tiefer Graben

Haydn

This ancient but rather depressing street (it means "deep ditch") was the scene of a youthful escapade of Haydn. For whatever reason he organised a large number of musicians to stand on the pavements of the Tiefer Graben with a timpanist positioned on the bridge above, which carries the Wipplingerstrasse over the Tiefer Graben. He then invited each of them to play a piece of their choosing simultaneously. The ensuing cacophony provoked an understandably furious reaction from the local residents. The police were also unimpressed by this early example of aleatoric music and arrested any musician they could lay their hands on. Haydn escaped.

24 I Tiefer Graben 18

Mozart

Having fallen into disrepair this house has been restored as the Hotel Tigra.

Mozart, then 17, and his father lived here from July until September 1773. The reason for the visit is not known, although it is probable that the objective was to secure an appointment for Mozart at the Imperial Court.

Mozart was granted an audience with Empress Maria Theresa in August but no appointment was forthcoming; Mozart was no longer a *wunderkind*, but yet another musician seeking employment.

He was not allowed to be idle; compositions here included his Serenade (K185), six string quartets (K168 – 173) and part of *Thamos, König in Ägypten.*

25 I Tiefer Graben 10

Beethoven

Beethoven lived on the floor of the "Greinersches Haus", which stood on this site, from early in 1800 until the spring of 1801.

A mosaic on the façade of the present building commemorates Beethoven's stay here, although it is a pity that the design for the mosaic was not proof-read before execution; the date is incorrect, also the opus numbers mentioned are a nonsense and have no connection with this property.

The works that Beethoven did compose here include the Piano Concerto No. 3 in C minor, the Horn Sonata (Opus 17) and the ballet *Prometheus*.

It was during Beethoven's stay here that there was a reference for the first time with regard to his hearing problems. In 1800 the nine-year-old Karl Czerny was brought to the apartment by his father with a view to becoming Beethoven's pupil. In his memoirs Czerny noted that Beethoven's ears were stuffed with cotton wool steeped in a yellow liquid.

26 I Renngasse 1

Schubert

This was the site of the "Römanischen Kaiser" inn, a small first-class hotel which had a hall which was used for concerts. In 1818 one of Schubert's overtures "In the Italian Style" was performed here.

Schubert at this time was much influenced by the operas of Rossini. It was the first orchestral work of Schubert to be given a public performance. The following year his song *Schäfers Klagenlied* was performed here. These events are recorded on the commemorative plaque.

Beethoven

Beethoven stayed at "Zum Römanischen Kaiser" temporarily in the winter of 1816-17. He was heavily involved in litigation with regard to the custody of his nephew Karl.

Wagner

In 1848 Wagner, with a warrant for his arrest still extant for his revolutionary activities in Dresden, stayed briefly in Vienna.

He was eager to meet the representatives of the Democratic Union of Vienna, and was taken to "Zum Römanischen Kaiser" to attend a meeting. The meeting, conducted by ill-educated and inarticulate officials, was a shambles and Wagner quickly took his leave.

27 I Freyung 6

Fux

This was the home of the Imperial Kapellmeister Johann Fux. Fux was a prolific composer and author of the famous treatise *Gradus ad Parnassum*.

The reputation of Fux as a dry academic is unfair. His music reveals great variety and melodic elegance and deserves to be better known.

28 Schottenkirche and Schottenhof

Haydn

Two weeks after Haydn's death a solemn Requiem Mass in his memory was celebrated in the Schottenkirche. The Requiem Mass was by Haydn's great friend Mozart.

In the late eighteenth century one of the apartments in the Schottenhof was occupied by Marianne von Genzinger, the wife of Prince Esterházy's personal physician. An intelligent, amusing and musically gifted woman, Marianne played hostess to the musical celebrities of the day. Guests at Sunday lunch included Haydn, Mozart, Dittersdorf and Albrechtsberger. That Haydn composed for her the difficult Piano Sonata No. 59 in E♭ is testimony to her skill as a pianist.

In Marianne the unhappily married Haydn found a good friend and sympathetic confidante. He was deeply moved by her death in 1793 at the age of 42.

Schubert

Another apartment in the Schottenhof was the home of Otto Hatwig who conducted rehearsals of the small orchestra which had developed from the family chamber music group in the Schubert household. (see XII: 8).

Among the orchestral works of Schubert that were played here was the Symphony No. 5 in B♭ in 1815.

Liszt

Liszt maintained an apartment in the Schottenhof between 1869 and 1886 (commemorated by a plaque). It was the office of his uncle Eduard, a lawyer. Among Eduard Liszt's clients was one Bertha Goldwag, an interior designer who had furnished Wagner's rooms at Penzing (see XVI: 6). After Wagner had fled his creditors (including Frau Goldwag), she consulted Herr Liszt about recovering her money.

Bruckner

The pious Bruckner was a regular worshipper at the Schottenkirche. (His home was in near-by Hessgasse (see XII: 15)).

At Easter in 1885 Brucker paid a courtesy call on Liszt in the Schottenkirche and presented the score of his second symphony with a request that Liszt become its dedicatee. Liszt agreed, although he had little time for either Bruckner or his music. (Bruckner's habit of addressing Liszt as "Your Grace" or similar grated on the older composer).

The much-travelled and overworked Liszt then forgot the score and left it behind in Vienna. When Bruckner found out he was deeply hurt and rescinded the dedication.

29 Harrach Palace

This palace was constructed at the end of the seventeenth century for the Bohemian Counts of Harrach. After a fire in 1702, serious damage during the second world war and many renovations, only the unassuming Herrengasse aspect resembles the original building.

Haydn

The Counts of Harrach also owned the castle and estate at Rohrau, Haydn's birthplace. Haydn's mother was a cook to the Harrach household.

Mozart

In October 1762 the Mozart family, including six-year-old Wolfgang, was driven by coach to the Harrach Palace where Mozart and his sister performed for Count Ferdinand Harrach between 4 and 6pm. They were then whisked away to repeat the performance at the home of another wealthy nobleman.

30 Kinsky Palace

This splendid, beautifully-proportioned house is the work of the architect Johann von Hildebrandt and was constructed early in the eighteenth century for the first owner, Count Daun.

Mozart

On his first visit to Vienna in 1762 at the age of six Mozart and his family paid two visits to this palace, although the annexe to the palace in which Mozart and his sister performed has long been demolished.

Beethoven

In 1784 the palace passed into the hands of the Kinsky family. Prince Ferdinand Kinsky was a good friend of Beethoven and the composer was a frequent guest at the palace.

In 1809 Beethoven received an offer from the King of Westphalia, Napoleon's brother Jerome, to become the kapellmeister in Kassel. Beethoven's friends were appalled and negotiated a contract, brokered by Countess Erdödy, under the terms of which Beethoven would receive an annuity on condition that he remained in Austria. Among the guarantors was Prince Kinsky. After Kinsky's death from a riding accident Beethoven saw fit to sue Kinsky's estate to ensure the continuity of his annuity.

Schubert

In 1827 Schubert accompanied Baron Schönstein to a musical evening at the palace given by Kinsky's widow Charlotte. Schönstein sang a programme consisting entirely of songs by Schubert. The aristocratic audience applauded the singer ecstatically, ignoring the composer. Embarrassed, Charlotte apologised to Schubert who reassured her that he preferred to be ignored as he was embarrassed by plaudits. He dedicated his songs Opus 96 to the Princess.

|31| I Schreyvogelgasse 1 (corner of Teinfaltstrasse)

Schubert

This is the site of the "Klepperställe" ("Nags' stables") which was the home of Schubert's staunchest friend Josef von Spaun. On January 28th 1828, the year of Schubert's death, the last of the so-called "Schubertiads" took place here, attended by a number of distinguished musicians including the violinist Ignaz Schuppanzigh.

On this occasion Schubert's Piano Trio in E^b was played.

Beethoven

Beethoven lived here for a short period after the French occupation late in 1809.

Beethoven

Beethoven lived here for two periods; from 1804 to 1808 and again from 1810 to 1814. The house was owned by the Pasqualati family. Beethoven changed lodgings frequently, often following altercations with landlords, and the length of his stays here says much about his relationship with Baron Pasqualati who was not only his landlord but also his friend and legal adviser.

Beethoven's first apartment here was on the fourth floor but for the remainder of his stays here he occupied an apartment on the third floor. (Between February and June 1814 he moved into a first floor apartment in the neighbouring "Bartensteinisches Haus" at Mölkerbastei 10, a house, which has since been demolished.)

Beethoven's occupation of these rooms was not without interruptions, but Baron Pasqualati always kept his room vacant during Beethoven's absences, knowing that the composer would return.

Beethoven's rooms had magnificent views over the glacis to the Vienna Woods. His one disagreement with Pasqualati was when he knocked through a wall on the other side, so that he could look eastward towards the Prater, without obtaining prior permission from his landlord.

Among the compositions associated with this house are Fidelio, the Violin Concerto in D, the Piano Concerto No. 4 in G, the Symphony No. 5 in C minor and the "Rasumovsky" quartets (Op 59).

The apartment on the fourth floor is now a museum dedicated to the composer. Perhaps the most evocative exhibit is a lock of Beethoven's hair, cut off *post-mortem*.

V Around the Hofburg Palace

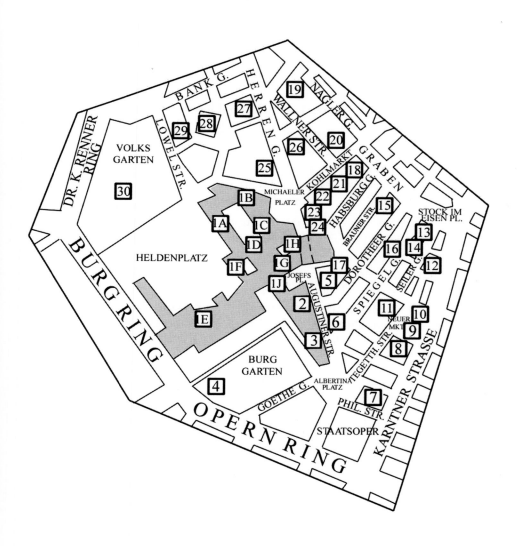

I The Hofburg Palace

For 600 years, until the collapse of the Habsburg Empire in 1918, the Hofburg Palace was the Imperial residence of the rulers of Austria.

The oldest section, dating from the thirteenth century, is the Schweizerhof (Swiss Court). The palace was progressively enlarged over the centuries by successive Emperors. Today it is an asymmetric complex of buildings in a miscellany of architectural styles.

A.   Leopoldinischer Tract (Leopold Wing)

This wing, completed in the seventeenth century, is today occupied by the President of Austria. In the eighteenth century the Empress Maria Theresa and her family lived in this wing where, in October 1762, the 6-year-old **Mozart** and his sister entertained the youngest Archdukes, Ferdinand and Maximilian Franz.

In January 1768 the Mozarts were granted an audience with the Empress here. Probably at the prompting of Leopold Mozart, the Empress's son and co-regent Josef II suggested that Wolfgang might compose an opera. Three months later Mozart, then 12, completed *La Finta Semplice*. Hopes of an early production were thwarted by intrigues involving the impresario Signor Affligio. Incandescent with rage Leopold petitioned the Emperor to no avail; the opera was not performed during this Viennese visit.

In 1773 **Mozart** and his father were in Vienna seeking an appointment at court. (see IV: 24). They were granted an audience with the Empress but "she was gracious and no more than that".

B.   Reichskanzleitract (Treasury Wing)

Here were the apartments of Emperor Franz Josef I and the Empress Elizabeth. They are open to the public.

Among the musicians given an Imperial Command to attend the audience chamber was **Dvořák**. In May 1889 the Emperor invested him with the Order of the Iron Crown.

C. Burgtheater

A commemorative plaque on the eastern side of the entrance on the Michaelerplatz marks the site of the former Burgtheater (Imperial theatre). In 1741 the ballroom of the Imperial Court was converted into a theatre which was eventually demolished in 1888. It was probably the disastrous fire at the Ringtheater on the Schottenring in 1881, claiming over 400 lives, which persuaded the Emperor that it was inadvisable to have a theatre attached to his home. The present Burgtheater on the Dr Karl Lueger Ring is freestanding and devoted to drama.

The old Burgtheater witnessed some of the most important events in the history of music.

Gluck's operas *Orpheus ed Eurydice, Alceste and Paride ed Elena* were premièred here, as were **Mozart's** *Entführung,* "The Marriage of Figaro" and *Così fan Tutte.*

When **Cimarosa** directed the first performance of *Il Matrimonio Segreto* (The Secret Marriage) in February 1792 Leopold II enjoyed it so much that he ordered supper for the cast and then a complete encore. Thus it is probably the only opera in history to receive its first and second performances on the same evening.

The first (public) performance of **Haydn's** "Creation" took place here in March 1799 to great acclaim.

Beethoven made his Viennese début as a composer/pianist here in March 1795, playing his Piano Concerto No. 2 in B^b . In April 1800 he directed the première of his first symphony in a concert which also included his Septet.

D. Schweizerhof (Swiss Wing)

Mozart appeared here on two occasions in 1781 shortly after his break with the Archbishop of Salzburg (see II : 2).

On November 16th he was invited to entertain the Duke of Württemberg and his family.

On Christmas Eve 1781 Emperor Josef II sponsored a piano "contest" between Mozart and Muzio Clementi before the Emperor and the Grand Duchess Maria Feodorovna. The "contestants" were required to play and improvise on a theme by Paisiello and also to play pieces of their own choosing. Mozart apparently gave a splendid account of himself even though one of the pianos was out of tune and three of its keys stuck!

Mozart, who never suffered musical fools gladly, was dismissive of Clementi's playing. In a letter to his father he described Clementi as a mere "mechanicus", one who plays with accuracy but without taste or feeling. This verdict would appear unfair; Clementi was a distinguished pianist and composer and was a founding member of the Philharmonic Society of London.

E.   Sammlung alter Musikinstrumente (Collection of old musical instruments)

Neue Burg (entrance in Heldenplatz)

This fascinating collection is housed in spacious although gloomily-illuminated rooms in the central section of the Neue Burg.

Founded at the end of the sixteenth century, the collection includes instruments from four centuries, most restored to working order. The exhibits were supplemented by the collection of the Gesellschaft der Musikfreunde which is permanently on loan here.

Among the items on display are the Érard piano played by Beethoven, the tablepiano used by Schubert and the Graf piano of Robert and Clara Schumann which they later gave to Brahms who in turn donated it to the Gesellschaft.

F.   Burgkapelle

The beautiful and intimate Imperial Chapel was constructed in the fifteenth century and has subsequently been modified on many occasions.

Among the distinguished musicians employed here were **Fux, Salieri, Gluck** and **Bruckner.** The Bohemian composer **Jan Václav Vořišek** was appointed court organist in 1822 in preference to, among others, **Franz Schubert**. After Voříšek's death in 1825 Schubert applied for the post of vice-kapellmeister and court organist, once again to no avail.

Bruckner was appointed to the post of organist-designate and teacher of the boy choristers in 1868. The post was an honorary one. In the previous year he had applied unsuccessfully for a post at the chapel even though **Johann Herbeck** (see III : 16) had conducted an acclaimed performance of Bruckner's Mass in D minor here.

A surprising nomination for the post of Hofkapellmeister in 1846 was **Hector Berlioz**, but the French composer would not consider moving from Paris.

In 1498 the Vienna Boys' Choir (see VI : 17) was founded to participate in the musical life of the chapel. Schubert was a member from 1808 to 1813. The choir, supplemented by members of the Vienna State Opera and accompanied by instrumentalists from the Vienna Philharmonic Orchestra, still takes part in Sunday morning sung Mass from September to June.

Visitors to the Sunday morning Mass often express disappointment that the choristers, seated in a high balcony, are not in view. However after the service the choristers, with good humour and patience beyond their years, stand smiling for endless photographs by tourists.

G.   Redoutensaal

The Redoutensäle occupy one side of the elegant Josefsplatz. The two rooms (large and small) were badly damaged by a major fire in 1992 and restoration work took several years.

The Redoutensaal takes its name from the great balls which were held here during the winter months in the late eighteenth and early nineteenth centuries. Berlioz proclaimed the large hall as "excellent for music".

As "I and R Chamber Composers" **Gluck** and his successor **Mozart** were obliged to supply dances for the court masked balls held in the two rooms.

In 1828 **Josef Lanner** was appointed Music Director of the Redoutensäle, reflecting the current musical predilection of the

Viennese. From 1831 the role was shared with **Johann Strauss (father)**. After Lanner's death Strauss petitioned the Emperor to confer upon him the honorary title K.K.Hofballmusik-Director.

In due course this title was passed on in turn to Strauss's eldest son Johann and then his youngest, Eduard. After Eduard's retirement on 1901 the title was given to **Carl Ziehrer.**

The Redoutensäle, were the venues of a number of important musical events. Among the most noteworthy were:-

In 1793, in the small hall, **Haydn** conducted three of his "London Symphonies".

In 1795 **Haydn** directed a performance of **Beethoven's** Piano Concerto No. 2 in B^b with the composer as soloist.

Haydn also gave the first (public) performance of his oratorio "The Seasons" in the large hall in 1801.

During the Congress of Vienna in 1814 **Beethoven** gave a concert in the Redountensaal at which all of the visiting monarchs were present. The programme included *Der glorreiche Augenblick* (The Glorious Moment).

Franz Liszt made his Viennese début at the age of 11 in the small hall. His final concert was 52 years later at the same venue in order to raise funds to aid flood victims in his native Hungary.

Paganini gave a series of concerts in the large hall (which seated 1000 people) in 1828. His demonic style of violin-playing induced "Paganini fever" among the Viennese.

Much less successful in 1831 was **Chopin**. His concert at the Redoutensaal at which he played a solo arrangement of his Piano Concerto in E minor attracted little attention.

Much better received was **Berlioz** who conducted a series of concerts in 1845. He returned to the large hall in 1866 to conduct an acclaimed performance of "The Damnation of Faust".

The Gesellschaft de Musikfreunde gave concerts in the small hall in 1815-16 but with the membership increasing were obliged to move to the larger hall where they were held until 1847.

In 1867 the first three movements of "A German Requiem" by **Brahms** were given here, conducted rather unsympathetically by Johann Herbeck (see III : 16). Herbeck allowed the great fugue in the third movement to be drowned by an over-enthusiastic timpanist.

H.   Winterreitschule (Winter Riding School)

This splendid hall was built between 1729 and 1735. Today it is graced by the elegant precision of the Lipizzaner stallions of the Spanish Riding School.

Between 1812 and 1816 the Gesellschaft der Musikfreunde sponsored a giant Musikfeste here before audiences of several thousand. The large choir and orchestra (mostly amateur) gave oratorios (usually by Handel).

J.   Österreichische National-bibliothek

(Austrian National Library)

This beautifully-proportioned building with its magnificent Grand Hall (the Prunksaal) was completed in 1735 and was originally free-standing.

In 1777 Baron Gottfried von Swieten was appointed Director of the Imperial Library. Von Swieten was an erudite man with a deep passion for music and a reputation for pedantry and parsimony. He had a profound love of the music of Bach and Handel, and was also an occasional composer (see VI : 16). In 1786 von Swieten founded a "Society of Associates" to promote his favourite music. Concerts were given each Sunday at noon in the Great Hall. **Mozart** became a frequent visitor to the library, in which von Swieten had an apartment. **Mozart** arranged the music of Handel, including "Messiah" and "Acis and Galatea", for the musical forces available, and conducted some of the concerts.

Von Swieten was a patron of **Mozart**. When his popularity declined Mozart found that his concert subscription list had dwindled to just one name – that of von Swieten.

The Baron also made the arrangements for Mozart's funeral. He opted for a third-class funeral, a decision for which posterity has judged him harshly.

After his retirement from Esterházy **Haydn** was a frequent visitor to the library. Von Swieten provided German translations of the texts which Haydn set in the "Seven Last Words", "The Creation" and "The Seasons".

Von Swieten was a patron of the young **Beethoven** who was also a frequent guest here. Beethoven dedicated his first symphony to his ageing benefactor.

2   Augustinerkirche

Schubert

On December 23rd 1828 a memorial service was held here for Franz Schubert who had died just over a month before. The Requiem Mass in C minor by Schubert's friend Anselm Hüttenbrenner was performed.

Bruckner

In 1872 Bruckner conducted the first performance of his Mass No. 3 in F minor to the approbation of Liszt and Brahms, who were also present.

Suppé

The funeral of Franz von Suppé took place at the Augustinerkirche in May 1895. The choirs of the two theatres with which Suppé had been associated, the Carltheater (see VI:23) and the Theater an der Wien (see X:4) took part, singing Suppé's *Ruhe Müder Wanderer*.

3   Albertina

The Department of Music of the National Library is housed on the top floor. This astonishing collection comprises nearly 50,000 items. Pride of place is given to the original score of Mozart's Requiem. Other gems are the scores of Beethoven's Violin Concerto, the "St Anthony Variations" by Brahms and *Der Rosenkavalier* by Richard Strauss.

Manuscripts dating from medieval times, and scores of music from Monteverdi to Berg are held here.

4   Mozart Monument, Burggarten

This familiar, rather romanticised, memorial by Viktor Tilgner dates from 1896. It originally stood in Albertinaplatz.

5   Palais Pálffy (I Josefsplatz 6)

Mozart

Wolfgang (aged 6) and his sister played for Count Nikolaus Pálffy, the Hungarian Chancellor, in October 1762.

It is also claimed that Mozart played through "The Marriage of Figaro", prior to the opera's première, in the so-called "Figarosaal".

6   Palais Lobkowitz (I. Lobkowitzplatz 2)

This imposing baroque mansion was the home of Prince Franz Josef Lobkowitz. A passionate music-lover, Lobkowitz employed his own private orchestra.

Haydn

Haydn was a frequent performer at the house. Lobkowitz commissioned Haydn's last completed quartets (Op77).

Beethoven

Many works by Beethoven were performed for the first time in the Prince's fine music room on the first floor. It is known as the "Eroicasaal" in recognition that in this beautifully-decorated room Beethoven's 3rd Symphony received its first performance at a private concert.

Lobkowitz was a co-guarantor of the contract granting Beethoven an annuity (see IV:30), an arrangement which ended abruptly in 1811 when the Prince was bankrupted; ruined by profligate spending on his orchestra and the financial consequences of the Napoleonic Wars.

7   The Sacher Hotel (Philharmonikerstrasse)

The legendary Sacher Hotel has stood here since 1876. After

protracted litigation with its rival Demel's, it is accepted as the home of the original Sachertorte. In the nineteenth century young army officers entertained young ladies from the Corps de Ballet in discreet *chambres privées*.

On special occasions Theodor Billroth, the distinguished surgeon, musical amateur and friend of **Brahms** (see XII : 4) invited the composer to the Sacher for oysters, champagne and asparagus. One such dinner was after the first Viennese performance of the Symphony No. 4 in E minor in January 1886. To Brahms it must have seemed a far cry from his early days living by the docks in Hamburg.

The Kärntnertor Theatre

Approximately on the site of the present Sacher Hotel stood the Kärntnertor Theatre were Mozart directed a performance of his Symphony No. 34 in C at a charity concert in 1781.

In 1810 it became the Imperial Opera House, (the Burgtheater reverting to the performance of drama). Among the premières at the Kärntnertor theatre were **Weber's** *Euryanthe. Linda di Chamounix* and *Maria di Rohan* by Donizetti and Flotow's Martha also received their first performances here.

It was at this theatre that there took place in May 1824 perhaps the most famous orchestral concert in musical history when Beethoven introduced his Choral Symphony.

When the present opera house was constructed as part of the Ringstrasse development in 1869 the Kärntnertor Theatre, by then too small and old fashioned, was demolished.

8   Neuer Market

Corner Tegetthofstrasse 8/Marco d'Aviano gasse 1

Here stood the town palace of Prince Schwarzenberg – it was demolished in 1894 and replaced by three apartment houses. In this palace **Haydn** gave the first performances of "Creation" in 1798 and "The Seasons" in 1801.

9   I Neuer Markt 2

Haydn

A commemorative plaque marks the site of the house in which Haydn lived from 1795 to 1797 while his new house in present-day Haydngasse (see X : II) was undergoing alterations. Here he composed the Austrian National Anthem (today that of Germany). The house was demolished in 1894.

10   I Neuer Markt 5

Mozart

Where the elegant Ambassador Hotel now stands was a former flour market that had been converted into a casino, the Mehlgrube. A large room in the casino was used as a concert hall. In 1785 Mozart gave a series of highly successful subscription concerts here, for each of which he composed a new piano concerto. The first concert, at which his amazed and delighted father was present, included the Piano Concerto No. 20 in D minor (K466).

11   I Neuer Markt 15

Köchert's jewellery shop

Wolf

Heinrich Köchert was the Imperial Jeweller, a wealthy man with powerful friends and one of Vienna's most notable cuckolds of the late nineteenth century.

The Köcherts invited the impecunious Hugo Wolf into their home, a kindness which Wolf repaid by seducing Köchert's wife Melanie.

Melanie remained devoted to Wolf even during the composer's final illness, syphilis – induced insanity, which necessitated the removal of Wolf to an asylum (see XII : 8)

After Wolf's death in 1903 Melanie suffered severe clinical depression. Three years later she threw herself from a fourth-floor window here and plunged to her death on the pavement below.

I Seilergasse 9

Fux

The Imperial Kapellmeister Johann Fux lived in a former house on this site from 1702 –15.

13 **I Spiegelgasse 9**

Schubert

The commemorative plaque records that Schubert lived here in the "Göttweigerhof" from early 1822 until the summer of 1825 and that in this house he composed his Symphony No. 8 in B minor, "The Unfinished".

He stayed here as a guest of his friend Franz von Schober (see IV : II) and his family . At some point during his stay here Schubert contracted syphilis. It was probably whilst accompanying the amoral Schober on one of his excursions to a local brothel that Schubert came into contact with the disease. It would blight the six years of life remaining to him.

The Enigma of the "Unfinished Symphony"

Schubert composed his eighth symphony apparently in appreciation of being made an honorary member of the Styrian Musical Society in Graz, and sent the manuscript to his friend Anselm Hüttenbrenner who lived there. Hüttenbrenner retained the score and it was not mentioned again for forty years. Then Johann Herbeck persuaded Hüttenbrenner to hand over the symphony, which was finally performed in 1865 in the Redoutensaal. The manuscript delivered by Hüttenbrenner comprised two movements and the first 21 bars (fully-scored) of the scherzo.

Modern scholarship leans to the view that the symphony was indeed unfinished. If so, why? The two most frequently postulated hypotheses are :-

A) That after completing two movements of the utmost sublimity Schubert was unable to maintain the same level of intensity and unity in the scherzo.

B) *Psychological problems upon contracting a venereal disease prevented Schubert from completing the work.*

There are other works of high quality which Schubert also failed to complete, notably his cantata "Lazarus" and the "Quartetsatz" D703.

Those who believe that the symphony was finished but that parts were lost make the valid point that Schubert was unlikely to send a "torso" to Graz. Hüttenbrenner's long silence about the work may indicate guilt that he had misplaced the last two movements.

Gerald Abraham has put forward an ingenious idea, although it has found little favour with musicologists. He suggests that when preparing incidental music to "Rosamunde" in 1823, pressed for time, Schubert lifted the finale from the symphony and it became the B minor entr'act in "Rosamunde".

14   I Spiegelgasse 11

Salieri

The plaque on this building (of more recent date) states misleadingly that Antonio Salieri lived and died here in 1825. Salieri at the end of his life was transferred to "secure accommodation" in the General Hospital in the Alsergrund (see XII : 9), where he died.

15   I Dorotheergasse 10

Doblinger's music – publishing house

A wide range of books on music and musical scores are on sale here. Doblinger's published music by **Mahler** and **Bruckner** and also by operetta composers such as **Ziehrer** and **Lehár**.

Doblinger's also encouraged contemporary composers such as **Zemlinsky**.

On the first floor is a charming intimate concert room where recitals are given before invited audiences.

16   I Dorotheergasse 9

Conradin Kreutzer

A plaque commemorates the residence here of the German composer and conductor Conradin Kreutzer. He was conductor for many years at the Kärntnertor Theatre (see V : 7).

His most successful opera was *Das Nachtlager von Granada*.

17   I Dorotheergasse 16 - 18

Protestant churches

Berg

At this church, dating from 1784, **Alban Berg** married Helene Nahowski in May 1911.

Lutheran Church (Dorotheergasse 18)

Brahms

The funeral of Brahms on April 6th 1897 was the most spectacular that Vienna had witnessed since that of Beethoven 75 years before.

Thousands lined the street as the cortège made its way from the Karlsgasse (see VI : 3) to the church where clergy and city dignitaries awaited.

The choir sang Mendelssohn's *Es its bestimmt in Gottes' Rath*.

Johann Strauss (son)

Two years later – on June 6th 1899 – all Vienna turned out to witness the funeral procession of Johann Strauss (son). The cortège passed the Theater an der Wein, the Musikverein and the Imperial Court Opera along streets lined by huge silent crowds.

In an emotionally-charged service, Strauss's body was consecrated here.

Schoenberg

In March 1898, Arnold Schoenberg converted to Protestantism here, and in this church in 1901 he married Mathilde von Zemlinsky, sister of the conductor and composer.

18   I Graben 17

Mozart

In 1905 the present nondescript building replaced the apartment house in which Mozart had a third-floor apartment from September 1781 until July 1782, shortly before his marriage to Constanze Weber.

He had been forced to leave the Weber household nearby (see IV : 7) by gossips speculating on his relationship with Constanze. Here Mozart completed *Die Entfüthrung aus dem Serail* which was premièred at the Burgtheater (see V : 1.C) in July 1782.

He also composed here the Symphony No. 35 in D major ("The Haffner").

19   I Naglergasse 9

Schoenberg

On this site was a building housing the school of Eugenia Schwarzwald, a pioneering educationalist and philanthropist.

In 1903 **Schoenberg** began to give lectures on harmony and counterpoint here. His new pupils included **Weben** and **Berg**. **Zemlinsky** also taught at the school.

In 1918 Schoenberg returned to preside over composition seminars. He also founded here the "Society for Private Musical Performances" as a forum for contemporary music.

20   I Wallnerstrasse 4 (Esterházy Palace)

Haydn

This splendid mansion was constructed in 1698 and was the Viennese residence of the Princes of Esterházy. Haydn played frequently in the small chapel.

Haydn was appointed assistant conductor of the Esterházy music ensemble by the music-loving Prince Paul Anton Esterházy in 1761. His first compositions for his new employer, symphonies 6, 7 and 8 (*Le Matin, Le Midi* and *Le Soir*) were performed in the Grand Salon in Wallnerstrasse.

21 I Kohlmarkt 7

Mozart

In 1784 Mozart and his wife Constanze moved temporarily to an apartment in the house which then stood on this site. With considerable understatement, Mozart described these lodgings as "uninspiring".

Here Mozart composed his "Masquerade" – a pantomime with music (K446) which Mozart, dressed as a harlequin, performed with friends at a public masked ball in the Redoutensaal.

22 I Kohlmarkt 9

Chopin

A commemorative plaque marks the site of the house in which Chopin stayed from November 1830 until July 1831. The house was demolished in 1900.

Chopin occupied three rooms on the third floor which he described as "splendid and elegantly furnished". But this visit to Vienna by Chopin, his second, was far less successful than his first two years earlier.

The house was owned by the famous publisher of music, Artaria, who numbered Mozart and Beethoven among his clients. The business is still in existence on the first floor of a more recent building on this site.

23 I Kohlmarkt 11

Michaelerhaus

Haydn

Haydn lived in a "miserable garret" here from 1750 to 1755. He had been released by St Stephen's choir after his voice broke (see I).

Virtually penniless, the 16-year-old Haydn was grateful enough to find the attic room, even though the roof leaked and he had no stove.

In more salubrious accommodation on the main floors of the house lived the Court Poet Metastasio (librettist of Mozart's *La Clemenza di Tito*), the mother of his future employer, Countess Esterházy and the composer and teacher Nikolaus Porpora.

Porpora employed Haydn as his accompanist, and Haydn learnt much from the older composer.

24 I Michaelerplatz 5

Constanza Mozart

After Mozart's death in 1791 his widow moved a number of times before leaving Vienna for good; her last residence was on the fourth floor here.

She had met a minor Danish diplomat, Georg Nissen, who she would eventually marry in 1809. They were apparently sharing this apartment, but the moral climate at the end of the eighteenth century made it imperative to keep their relationship discreet.

25 I Herrengasse 5

Palace Wilczek

Mozart

In 1762 6-year-old Mozart and his sister played for Count Johann Wilczek in this palace with the rather forbidding façade.

26 I Herrengasse 8

Site of the Bösendorfersaal

In Prince Liechtenstein's former riding school Ludwig

Bösendorfer (the son of the famous piano manufacturer) ran a small but elegant concert hall, demolished in 1913.

The plaque on the present building mentions only **Liszt** as a performer here; **Brahms, Mahler, Anton Rubinstein** and many virtuosi also performed in this hall.

In 1881 the String Quintet in F major by **Bruckner** was given here (without the finale) by a quintet led by Josef Hellmesberger.

In February 1907 an extraordinary concert took place here during which **Schoenberg's** String Quartet in D minor was premièred. At some point during the performance a member of the audience shouted abuse at Schoenberg, which prompted an outburst of hissing and catcalls. Gustav Mahler, by now the Director of the Court Opera, stood and remonstrated with the hecklers.

One of them lunged at Mahler, and but for the intervention of the artist Karl Moll, there would have been a brawl, and Vienna would have witnessed the startling sight of the Director of the Opera engaged in a bout of fisticuffs.

27   I Herrengasse 13

Landhaus

This sixteenth century palace dominates Herrengasse. The Gesellschaft der Musikfreund's Thursday evening concerts were often held in the Grand Hall during the early nineteenth century. **Schubert** figured predominantly at some of these concerts, as did **Beethoven** and **Liszt**.

28   I Minoretenplatz

Minoretenkirche

Salieri

This fourteenth century Gothic church with its beautiful portal serves the Italian Community as it has since 1784.

In June 1816 Salieri celebrated the 50th anniversary of his arrival in Vienna. The festivities began in this church where Salieri, his four daughters and many friends and pupils, including Schubert, heard mass.

29   I Löwelstrasse 6

Beethoven

Beethoven lived on the first floor of this house from May 1795 until February 1796. He had arrived in Vienna in 1792 relatively unknown and it is a sign of the rapid increase in his reputation that only three years later he was invited to compose music for the Annual Ball for the pension fund of the Society of Artists held at the Redoutensaal. Thus Beethoven composed the twelve minuets (W.07) and twelve German dances (W.08) in this house. It is also probable that it was here that he composed his beautiful song *Adelaide*.

30   Volksgarten

After the destruction of the Burg bastion during the French bombardment of 1809 a park was created in which the Viennese could stroll in civilised surroundings. It opened in 1823.

Orchestras were a feature of the gardens, in particular that of **Johann Strauss (father)**. Two days later after his father's funeral in 1849 **Johann Strauss (son)** conducted his father's orchestra here for the first time.

It was Strauss who first introduced the Viennese to Wagner's *Tristan and Isolde*, deemed unperformable at the Opera. Strauss played selections from the opera in the Volksgarten.

When Strauss died in June 1899, it was at the Volksgarten that news of his death became known. During a concert to raise funds for a Strauss-Lanner memorial, a message was passed to the conductor. He stopped the orchestra and then played "The Blue Danube". The audience stood and then quietly drifted away. No words were necessary.

VI Leopoldstadt

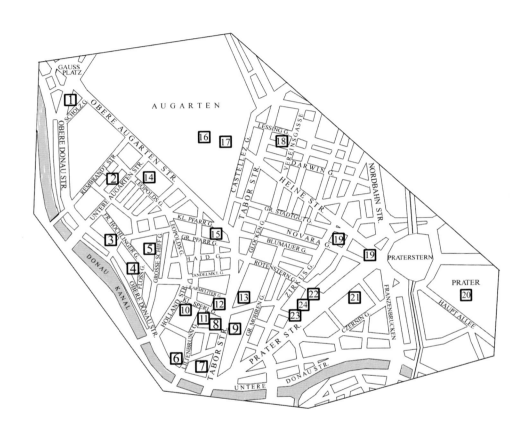

1   II Obere Donaustrasse 5

Schoenberg

Arnold Schoenberg was born in this house in September 1874. Schoenberg's parents were Jewish but his father was very much a "free-thinker" which may have influenced Schoenberg to convert to Protestantism (see V: 17).

2   II Untere Augartenstrasse 27

Oscar Straus

The operetta composer Oscar Straus was born and brought up in the house which preceded the present building. In his youth he was friendly with Schoenberg who lived nearby. He trained with Max Bruch in Berlin as a classical composer, but his operas and chamber music were eclipsed by his popular operettas, notably the "Waltz Dream" and *"Die Lustigen Niblungen"*.

He was also a conductor at the Carltheater (see VI: 24).

3   II Obere Donaustrasse 57

Suppé

Franz von Suppé lived in an apartment here from 1862 to 1865. He lived alone; he had separated from his first wife Therese, who would die in 1865. Here he composed his operettas *"Zehn Mädchen und kein Mann"* and *"Flotte Bursche"*. He had been appointed conductor at the nearby Theater am Franz-Josefs Kai. His position became spectacularly redundant when the theatre burnt to the ground in 1863.

4   II Flossgasse 7

Johann Strauss (father)

A plaque marks the site of the beer tavern "Zum Heiligen Florian" which stood here until its demolition in 1906. Here in March 1804 was born Johann Strauss, the father of the "waltz dynasty".

5   II Grosse Schiffgasse 21

Fritz Kreisler

In this house in February 1875 was born the legendary violinist Fritz Kreisler. He was enrolled as a student at the Vienna Conservatoire at seven and toured the United States as a virtuoso at 15. On his return to Vienna he entered medical school but gave up his medical studies to follow a musical career. There are a number of compositions of Kreisler which are still in the violin repertoire, in particular his cadenza for the Beethoven Violin Concerto.

In his youth he frequented coffee houses and played music with Schoenberg.

6   II Obere Donaustrasse 93-5

Dianabad

The present Dianabad is the fourth public swimming bath on this site. The original Dianabad opened in 1810. Every winter it was converted into a ballroom, the famous "Dianasaal".

In February 1867 *An der schönen blauen Donau* ("The Blue Danube") was heard for the first time here, although its composer, Johann Strauss (son) was conducting elsewhere that evening. It had been composed as a choral waltz for the influential Vienna Men's Choral Society. The text, provided by the Society's "house-poet", was absurd and the first performance was followed by just one encore – poor by the standards of Strauss at this time.

In 1862 Eduard Strauss made his début as conductor of his brother's orchestra here. The following year Carl Ziehrer launched his career with his own orchestra in the Dianasaal.

7   II Tabor Strasse 11

Josef Strauss

Here stood the last residence of Josef Strauss, the second of three musical sons of Johann Strauss (father). After their marriage Josef and Caroline Strauss moved into the Strauss family home, the Hirchenhaus (see VI: 8). Although they longed to move away from the family it was not until after the birth of their only child Karolina Anna that they could afford to do so.

In 1870 Josef left his wife and child here while he travelled to conduct a concert in Warsaw. He collapsed at the podium and was brought back to the Hirshenhaus where he died a month later, possibly from a brain tumour. He was 42.

After his death his brother Johann said simply: "Josef was the more gifted, I was merely more popular".

| 8 | II Taborstrasse 17 |

Hirschenhaus

Strauss family

Zum goldenen Hirsch, a large four-storied apartment building, was for a long time the family home of the Strauss family. Johann Strauss (father) moved to rooms on the second floor in 1834 with his wife Anna. Here Eduard Strauss, the third of the musical brothers was born.

After his separation from Anna, Strauss left the Hirschenhaus and moved in with his mistress in a house in Kumpfgasse (see III: 2).

In this house Josef Strauss died in 1870 (see VI: 7). In another apartment in the Hirschenhaus lived Anton Strauss (no relation), his wife Adèle and two year old daughter Alice. At 26 Adèle was widowed; she would become the third wife of Johann Strauss (son).

Eduard was the last Strauss to leave the house in 1886.

| 9 | II Taborstrasse 16-18 |

Kirche der Barmherzigen Brüder (Church of the Compassionate Brothers)

Haydn

After leaving the choir of St. Stephen's at 16 Haydn lived in an attic in the Michaelerhaus (see V: 23) eking out a living as best he could. Between 1755 and 1758 he was employed as organist and leader of the orchestra at this church.

10   **II Kleine Sperlgasse 2a-2c**

Zum Sperl

The "Sperl" was an abbreviation of "Zum Sperlbauer" and should not be confused with the "Sperl" coffee-house in Gumpendorferstrasse (see IX: 6).

"Zum Sperl" opened its doors in 1807. It included a garden area and a public dance hall, sumptuously decorated. **Johann Strauss (father)** and **Lanner** performed here frequently. In 1849 Strauss played here for the last time; six days later he died.

As the Dianabad-Saal became increasingly popular "Zum Sperl" began a slow decline into disrepute. In 1873 it was closed and the building demolished.

11   **II Kleine Sperlgasse 10**

Sechter

This was the residence of Simon Sechter, the Court organist, composer and renowned teacher. In 1828 Schubert approached Sechter for lessons in counterpoint, presumably with a view to acquiring a position at the Burgkapelle where improvisations of a fugal nature were *de rigueur*.

Bruckner also came here twice weekly for instruction in counterpoint, an arrangement that continued for some years.

Other pupils of Sechter were Suppé and Josef Strauss.

12   **II Karmeliterplatz**

Karmeliterkirche

This seventeenth century church is now known as St. Josef's. In 1805 Schubert's father applied unsuccessfully for the post of kapellmeister here.

Among its Kapellmeister it numbered **Albrechtsberger** (see II: 5), who taught Beethoven. In 1792 a pupil of Albrechtsberger, **Josef Eybler** became kapellmeister after testimonials were submitted by both his teacher and Mozart.

It was to Eybler that Constanza Mozart first turned with a request to complete the Requiem. Eybler added a few bars (which are still to be seen on Mozart's score in the Albertina Museum (see V: 3)), but then, for whatever reason, withdrew.

13   II Taborstrasse 48

Schoenberg

From Obere Donaustrasse 5 (see IV: 1) the Schoenberg family moved to this house. On New Year's Eve 1890 Schoenberg's father died, a victim of an influenza epidemic. With the family in straitened circumstances Schoenberg left school and was apprenticed as a bank clerk at Werner and Company at Wipplingerstrasse 39.

Now 16, Schoenberg fell in love for the first time. The young lady was his cousin Malvina who apparently found the earnest young Arnold not to her taste. She left Vienna and the romance fizzled out.

14   II Leopoldsgasse 9

Schoenberg

Schoenberg moved to this house in 1894. He was now 21 and had began to conduct men's choral societies having given up his position at the bank in order to concentrate on music. He was a cellist in an amateur orchestra, "Polyhymnia", which was conducted by Alexander von Zemlinsky, who also taught Schoenberg composition. While living here Schoenberg became involved with Zemlinsky's sister Mathilde who would become Schoenberg's first wife in 1901 (see V: 17).

In his String Quartet in D major (1897) Schoenberg began to stretch the limits of tonality. With his String Sextet *Verklärte Nacht*, composed in 1899, he moved into the realms of atonality.

15   II Grosse Pfarrgasse

Leopoldkirche

This eighteenth century church with its familiar tower was restored after serious bomb damage during the Second World War.

In 1796, the year before the birth of **Schubert,** his father applied unsuccessfully for the position of schoolmaster in the school associated with this church.

Both **Johann Strauss (son)** and his brother **Josef** sang in the choir here, an activity which had welcome financial benefits for their parents; their school fees at the prestigious "Schottengymnasium" were waived.

16 II Obere Augartenstrasse

Augartensaal

In the pavilion where the famous Augarten Porcelain is now produced, morning concerts, beginning at 8am, were given to celebrate the arrival of spring. For many years at the end of the eighteenth century and the first half of the nineteenth these morning concerts were a regular event each May.

In May 1782 **Mozart** gave a morning concert here. He directed a performance of his Symphony No. 34 in C (K338). He also played his Concerto for Two Pianos (K365) in which the other soloist was his pupil Josepha Auernhammer. This young lady was apparently seriously enamoured of her teacher, feelings which were not reciprocated. In a letter Mozart described her as "fat and ugly". She was, however, a fine pianist.

At this concert a symphony by Baron Gottfried von Swieten (see V: 1 J) was also played, although the score has been lost.

In May 1803 **Beethoven** gave the first performance of his Violin Sonata in A major (Op. 47) "The Kreutzer". The violinist was the exotically named George Polgreen Augustus Bridgetower, a violinist of mulatto extraction whose technique was greatly admired by Beethoven.

A commemorative plaque (often obscured by ivy) also notes that the charming part-song by **Schubert** *Die Nachtigall* (The

Nightingale) was also performed here in May 1824.

Wagner, who also came here, once remarked that the waltzes of Strauss "were more potent than alcohol". **Johann Strauss (son)** returned the compliment by playing arrangements of Wagner overtures here. Wagner's music was little known in Vienna at that time, and many Viennese were introduced to it by the performances of Strauss.

17   II Obere Augartenstrasse

Augartenpalais

This seventeenth century Baroque palace is today the boarding school of the Vienna Boys Choir. This world-famous choir was founded by Maximillian I to provide music for Masses in the Burgkapelle, a function which continues to this day (see V:1F).

Members of this 500-year-old tradition include Haydn, Schubert and the conductors Clemens Krauss and Felix Mottl.

At the end of the First World War this unique institution nearly folded; it was revived under private ownership. There are actually four choirs, each of 24 members, which allow participation in Sunday Mass at the Burgkapelle, concert work, recordings and also extensive tours.

To be admitted as a member of the "Wiener Sängerknaben" is an honour and a privilege. The schedule is very taxing; in addition to choir practices and performances, each boy is given tuition in playing an instrument and there is the normal strict academic régime in other subjects.

Through the railings the boys, in jeans and trainers instead of their familiar sailor-suits, can be seen in normal boyhood pursuits, football and skate-boarding.

18   II Vereingasse 21-23

Schoenberg

The present highly respected Bundesrealgymnasium was, in

Schoenberg's schooldays, a mediocre establishment. Schoenberg entered secondary school here in 1885 at the age of 11. He was not a particularly willing pupil and his academic record was average.

He left in 1891, without completing his diploma, when the death of his father (see VI: 13) compelled him to find paid employment.

| 19 | **II Novarragasse 39** |

| 19 | **Novarragasse 55** |

Brahms

Brahms arrived in Vienna in 1862, although it was a few years later before he decided to make the city his permanent home.

He lived in an apartment at No. 39 for a few months before moving to another apartment in the same street at No. 55 where he lived from 1862 to 1863.

The proximity of the Prater (see VI: 20) was a source of great pleasure to him and he enjoyed his walks there to the end of his days.

| 20 | **II Prater** |

The Prater is the six-mile-long tract of woodland and parkland between the Danube and the Danube canal. At its western end is the rather tawdry "Volksprater", a fun fair dominated by the Ferris Wheel of "The Third Man" fame which came into operation in 1897.

The Prater was formerly the Imperial Hunting Ground. In 1766 Josef II commanded that it be opened to the public. The arrow-straight "Hauptallee" became a favourite promenade of the Viennese.

Shortly after the opening of the Prater to the public three cafés were built, named rather unimaginatively "the First", "the Second" and "the Third". Groves of trees formed natural amphitheatres under which orchestras played. The Quintet of **Josef Lanner** was probably the first of these outdoor orchestras.

The "Third" café was, perhaps, the best-loved musical restaurant in Vienna. **Johann Strauss (father)** and later **Johann (son)** performed regularly here.

In 1814 **Beethoven** gave his last (and disastrous) public performance as a pianist here. His hearing had deteriorated to such an extent that he was unable to hear *piano* passages. In music marked forte he hammered the keys so ferociously that piano strings snapped. After this performance, in which he became hopelessly out of step with the other players, he retired as a concert pianist.

Entrepreneurial restaurateurs established a number of restaurants in the Prater. "Zum wilden Mann" was the scene of an unpleasant incident involving **Beethoven**. Soon after the first performance of the "Choral Symphony" in May 1824, Beethoven invited his factotum Anton Schindler and some friends to a meal at this restaurant. Beethoven arrived in a foul mood. The financial profit from the concert had not met his expectations and he accused Schindler and others of cheating him. Schindler, who had worked so hard to ensure the success of the concert, was appalled. He and the other guests left immediately leaving Beethoven to vent his anger on the hapless waiters.

Beethoven and, later, **Brahms** and **Schoenberg** were regular visitors to the Prater enjoying the wide spectrum of music on offer, ranging from military marches to arrangements of popular operas and operettas. The three cafés were destroyed during the closing days of the Second World War.

In October 1791 **Mozart**, tired, ill and depressed, was driven to the Prater in a carriage with his wife Constanza. Sitting in the park Mozart began to talk of death. He insisted that he had been poisoned by "acqua toffana", a concoction of arsenic, antimony and lead, and that the Requiem on which he was engaged was for himself. A horrified Constanza endeavoured to talk her husband out of his "black thoughts" but to no avail. With tears coursing down his cheeks he repeated that he would soon be dead. Six weeks later he died. The myths and legends surrounding Mozart's death thus were initiated in the Prater.

21 II Praterstrasse 54

Johann Strauss (son)

Johann Strauss lived with his wife Jetty in a first-floor apartment in this house from 1866 to 1868. Since 1978 it has been a museum devoted to Strauss and his music. There were many raised eyebrows in Vienna when the authorities gave permission for a burger restaurant to open on the ground floor.

Here Strauss composed *An der schönen blauen Donau* ("On the beautiful blue Danube").

22 Praterstrasse/Nepomukgasse

Johannes von Nepomuk Kirche (Church of St. John of Nepomuk).

Josef Strauss

Josef was the only one of the three sons of Johann Strauss (father) to have a conventional marriage. In June 1857 he married his long time girl-friend Karoline Pruckmayer in this church, which was then of fairly recent construction. As a wedding present he presented to his bride his affecting waltz *Perlen der Liebe* (Op 39).

23 II Praterstrasse 31

Site of the Carltheater

The Carltheater replaced an old Baroque theatre on this site (The Leopoldstadt Theatre) and opened in 1847 with **Suppé's** *Flötte Bursche*.

Suppé maintained his connection with the theatre until 1882. Among his operettas premièred here were Fatinitza and his masterpiece *Boccaccio*.

Suppé was influenced by another composer of operetta, **Jacques Offenbach**. Offenbach became a great favourite at the Carltheater, beginning in 1856 with *Le Mariage aux Lanternes*. This was followed by four more works by Offenbach in quick succession, played invariably to packed houses. His greatest success, inevitably, was with "Orpheus in the Underworld".

When **Johann Strauss (son)** began to compose operettas the Viennese anticipated a keen rivalry, which they would relish. (NB Strauss (father) v Strauss (son).) But Strauss and Offenbach were on friendly personal terms and there was never any animosity between them. Strauss directed the première of *Prinz Methusalem* here in 1877.

At the turn of the century **Zemlinsky** and **Oscar Straus** were both active here. A surprising substitute for Straus in 1901 was Schoenberg who conducted operettas at this theatre.

Franz Lehár's first great theatrical success, *Der Rastelbinder*, was premièred at the Carltheater in 1902.

The theatre's ventures into opera were less successful. When a mediocre Italian company played here in 1883 **Mahler** was enlisted to rehearse the chorus, with indifferent results.

In 1913 **Puccini** came here and received a substantial commission to compose a light opera in Straussian style. Puccini responded with *La Rondine*, but its production was delayed by the Great War. Eventually the première was staged in Monte Carlo. La Rondine has never established itself in the standard operatic repertoire.

The Carltheater was destroyed by bombing in 1944 and the site subsequently redeveloped.

24   II Praterstrasse 43

Johann Strauss (son)

Johann Stauss and his wife Jetty moved here in 1863 and lived here for about a year. (The original house no longer exists).

VII Landstrasse

[1] III Josef Gallgasse 6

Goldmark

The long life of Karl Goldmark came to an end in 1915 in the house which stood here. He was 84. Goldmark was a highly esteemed teacher in Vienna and was a friend of Brahms. His breakthrough as a composer came in 1875 with his opera "The Queen of Sheba". His "Rustic Wedding Symphony" and a lyrical Violin Concerto have remained in the recording repertoire.

[2] III Löwengasse 53a

Webern

Anton von Webern was born in this building on December 3rd 1883. He was the second of three surviving children and was baptised in the Roman Catholic faith. His father was a mining engineer. The family lived here until 1889 when a promotion for the father necessitated a move to Graz.

[3] III Marxergasse 17

Sofiensaal

In 1848 a Russian steam bath here was redeveloped into a large indoor swimming bath, the "Sofienbad", according to plans by Siccardsburg and Null. (Twenty years later, they designed the building which today is the Staatsoper (see XX)).

In common with the Dianabad-Saal (see IV: 6) there was a provision for covering the bath with a dance floor in winter. New salons were added together with galleries and expensive décor.

The Sofiensaal became a sumptuous ballroom in which members of the Strauss family were regular performers. In 1859 both **Johann Strauss (son)** and his brother **Josef** conducted their own orchestras alternately during an evening of non-stop dancing.

In 1864 both **Johann Strauss (son)** and **Offenbach** were invited by the Journalists' Society, the "Concordia" to compose waltzes for the annual Concordia Ball. Offenbach called his waltz *Abentblätter*

("Evening Papers") and Strauss was persuaded to name his *Morgenblätter* (Morning Papers).

It was in 1860 that Strauss composed his *Accellerationen* ("Accellerations") for the Engineering Students' Ball here. It is considered to be the first of Strauss's great mature waltzes.

In more recent times the Sofiensaal was converted into a major recording studio, in which the Vienna Philharmonic Orchestra has made a number of recordings.

On August 16th 2001 the Sofiensaal was devastated by fire, and only the blackened outer shell of the building remains. At the time of writing its future is very uncertain.

4 III Rasumovskygasse 29

Mozart

This was the home of Franz Mesmer, the distinguished physician who invented the concept of "animal magnetism", the precursor of hypnotism. He was a music-lover and a close friend of Mozart over a number of years.

In 1768 the first performance of the 12-year-old Mozart's little singspiel *Bastien und Bastienne* was given here, possibly in a garden pavilion.

In 1773 when Mozart, then 17, was in Vienna with his father, a "grand concert" was given in Mesmer's garden which probably included Mozart's Divertimento in D major (K205).

5 III Rasumovskygasse 23

Palais Rasumovsky

Beethoven

Count (later Prince) Andreas Rasumovsky was the wealthy Russian Ambassador to Vienna. He was a proficient amateur violinist who had taken lessons with Haydn.

At his sumptuous palace Rasumovsky founded a string quartet, led by Ignaz Schuppanzigh. Rasumovsky commissioned from Beethoven a set of string quartets, the "Rasumovsky Quartets" (Op 59) which were played for the first time here.

Beethoven also dedicated his fifth and sixth symphonies jointly to Rasumovsky and the Ambassador's brother-in-law Prince Lichnowsky who was Beethoven's first Viennese patron (see XII: 3).

After a banquet during the Congress of Vienna in 1814 the palace was gutted by fire but was soon restored to its former glory.

| 6 | **III Erdberg Strasse 19** |

Beethoven

In 1812 Beethoven wrote a passionate love-letter to a woman he addressed as "The immortal (or eternal) beloved". Her identity has been the subject of endless conjecture by Beethoven scholars since its discovery, together with the Heiligenstadt Testament (see XV: 8), among Beethoven's papers after his death. For reasons unknown Beethoven did not send the letter.

The distinguished American musicologist Professor Maynard Solomon has made a compelling case that the intended recipient of this letter was Antonie von Brentano. When her father died in 1809 she moved into his house here while she wound up his estate.

This was an unhappy period for Antonie; she was contemplating, with great reluctance, a move to Frankfurt with her husband Franz while still grieving for her father. Beethoven came here several times, often playing the piano to raise the spirits of Antonie who was frequently confined to bed by various illnesses.

In 1812 Beethoven composed a delightful little Piano Trio in B♭ for Antonie's 10-year-old daughter Maximilliane. To Antonie he dedicated his "Diabelli Variations".

The house was destroyed by bombing in the Second World War.

Professor Solomon's research has prompted much speculation on the nature of the relationship between Beethoven and Antonie von Brentano.

But there are two factors which, in the opinion of the author, preclude the likelihood of intimacy between them; they are, firstly, Beethoven's friendship with Antonie's husband Franz, and secondly Beethoven's well-documented prudish distaste for extra-martial affairs.

Further suggestions that Beethoven was the father of Antonie's son Franz Josef are based on evidence which is circumstantial to the point of wishful thinking.

7   III Erdberg Strasse 17

Schubert

This was the home of the radical but extremely popular Professor Heinrich Watteroth. A Viennese cardinal once attempted to ban one of his books because it defended Protestantism.

Two of Schubert's friends had rooms in this house; Josef von Spaun and Josef Witticzek (who would become Watteroth's son-in-law). In 1816 Schubert shared a room here with Spaun.

On Watteroth's name-day Schubert conducted his cantata *Prometheus* in the garden of Watteroth's house. (The score is lost). It was the first occasion that Schubert received remuneration for a composition.

As a prank his friends locked Schubert into a room in the tower and refused to release him until he produced a new work. Thus there came into being the *Écossaises* for piano (D421).

The house was severely damaged during World War II although the tower remains.

8   III Erdberg Strasse 1

Ziehrer

The house in which Carl Michael Ziehrer died on November 14th 1922 was also destroyed during the war. A plaque marks the site.

9   III Landstrasser Hauptstrasse 96

Brahms

A bronze plaque marks the site of the "Arenbergschlössl" which was demolished in 1958. It was the home of Dr. Richard Fellinger, a Viennese industrialist who lived here with his wife Maria and their three children. Brahms spent many happy hours here as a guest of the Fellinger family in the last years of his life. Maria Fellinger was a photographer and sculptor to whom Brahms scholars are indebted for the many informal photographs of the composer taken late in his life.

In this congenial and intellectually stimulating family circle Brahms found the stable and comfortable family life for which he yearned (but without the obligations and commitments which he feared). He spent each Christmas for the last seven years of his life here.

A number of works by Brahms were heard here for the first time including the Sonata for Piano and Cello in F (Op 99). The cellist on this occasion was Robert Hausmann, one of the leading exponents of the day, who lodged with the Fellingers.

Brahms was the recipient of many kindnesses on the part of the Fellingers. When Brahms's housekeeper died in 1886 it was Maria Fellinger who supervised the employment of a replacement, and the Fellingers also arranged for electric lighting to be installed in Brahms's apartment in the Karlsgasse (see IX: 3), an innovation that was not altogether to the composer's liking.

10   III Landstrasser Hauptstrasse 60

Beethoven

In the "Grosser Haus der Augustiner" which stood here Beethoven lived between 1820 and 1822 except for periods at Baden and at Döbling.

Here, in dingy rooms he worked on his last two Piano Sonatas, Op 110 in A^b and Op 111 in C minor.

It was to these rooms that Rossini came to pay a courtesy visit in April 1822. Rossini was so appalled by Beethoven's domestic squalor that he attempted unsuccessfully to arrange for a regular stipend for the morose composer.

11   III Landstrasser Hauptstrasse 75 – 77

Mozart

In April 1787 Mozart moved from his expensive lodgings in the Schulerstrasse (see III: 6) to a house which used to stand here. Although rather small the apartment faced the garden of which Mozart was able to take advantage.

This was an unhappy period for Mozart; he was suffering from a kidney complaint and his financial position was precarious. In May came news of the death of his father in Salzburg. Mozart also lost his pet starling, which he had bought in 1784 (see IV: 1). He buried it in the garden.

During his stay here Mozart composed part of *Don Giovanni*, which had been commissioned by the Estates Theatre in Prague. He also composed his *Eine Kleine Nachtmusik* in this house.

The Mozarts left in December 1787.

12   III Landstrasser Hauptstrasse 26

Beethoven

Beethoven lived in a second floor apartment in the house known as "Zum grünen Kranz" in 1817 and the first part of 1818. The apartment house was subsequently replaced by a new building. Beethoven interrupted his stay here in the summer months when he stayed in Heiligenstadt. It was not unusual for Beethoven to pay rent on two or more lodgings at the same time.

These were difficult times for Beethoven; having been awarded custody of his nephew Karl after a bitter and protracted battle against his sister-in-law Johanna, the boy's mother, Beethoven was attempting to gain the affection of Karl, with little success. He moved to this address to be close to the boy's school.

13   III Ungargasse 2

Brahms

Brahms lived in rooms in a hotel, which used to stand here "Zur goldenen Spinne". Brahms was deeply unhappy during his stay here. He had fallen in love with Julie Schumann, the daughter of his closest friend Clara Schumann. Fifteen years before, Brahms had been deeply in love with Julie's mother. Brahms kept his feelings from both Julie and, understandably, her mother. He was devastated when the announcement was made that Julie was to marry a minor Italian count. It was only when Brahms pushed the score of his *Alto Rhapsody* into her hands and told her it was his "bridal song" that Clara realised the reason for Brahms's strange behaviour at this time. Her reaction was not recorded.

While staying here Brahms was occupied by choral music, including the *Triumphlied* and the beautiful *Schicksalslied*.

At the beginning of 1872 he made the decision that Vienna would be his permanent home and he moved to an apartment in the Karlsgasse (see IX:3).

14   III Ungargasse 5

Beethoven

Beethoven lived in this house "Zur schönen Sklavin" in an apartment on the third floor. His nephew Karl lived with him at this time. The commemorative plaque records that Beethoven completed the "Choral Symphony" in this house.

He lived here from October 1823 until May 1824.

15   III Salesianergasse 12

Hugo von Hofmannsthal

The poet, playwright and librettist Hofmannsthal was born in this house in 1874. He was the librettist of a number of operas by Richard Strauss, including *Der Rosenkavalier*.

16

III Auenbruggergasse 2

Mahler

Otto Wagner, the leading architect in Vienna of his time, constructed this fine apartment house in 1891. In 1898 Mahler rented an apartment in this house on the third floor. He lived here firstly with his sister and then, after his marriage, with his wife Alma.

Mahler occupied this apartment until 1909. During this period he was Director of the Hofoper (see XX), the most prestigious position in music.

Among the regular guests here was Arnold Schoenberg who received considerable encouragement from Mahler, even though Mahler was somewhat nonplussed by Schoenberg's music.

In 1906 Mahler received a visit from nine-year-old Erich Korngold, a child prodigy. Mahler was astonished by the maturity of the child's compositions. Korngold became a respected composer of film music in America.

17

III Rechte Bahngasse 30-32

Schoenberg

In this large apartment building Schoenberg lived (with interruptions) from 1917 until 1924. It would be his last Viennese residence. He then moved to Berlin before, having witnessed vitriolic anti-Semitism by the rising Nazi régime in Germany, he left to live in exile in the United States for the rest of his life.

These were desperate times for Schoenberg; he was discharged from the army in 1917 because of health problems and was experiencing severe financial difficulties. In the last days of the Great War (and the Hapsburg Empire) food and other essentials were in short supply. In 1918 Schoenberg moved to the more congenial town of Mödling (see XVIII: C).

Schoenberg's plight was alleviated to some extent by monetary gifts from friends, in particular Webern and Mahler's widow Alma.

Concert life was much diminished and in any case was unsympathetic to Schoenberg's music. In 1918 he founded the Society for Private Musical Performance, a forum for contemporary music, which was played to sympathetic audiences.

In 1921 Schoenberg returned to Vienna. He had been experimenting with serial techniques for some time. In his Piano Suite (Op 25) he composed his first completely twelve-tone work, i.e. based on the twelve tones of the chromatic scale.

In 1923 Schoenberg's first wife Mathilde died, (see XI: 23). After his second marriage a year later he never returned here.

18 Rudolfsspital (Archduke Rudolf's Hospital)

Berg

In 1935 Alban Berg was bitten on his back by an insect. The bite became infected and Berg was admitted to this hospital. In those pre-antibiotic days the physicians were unable to prevent the onset of septicaemia and Berg died here on December 23rd 1935, a week after his admission, at the age of 50. The death mask was taken by Anna Mahler, the daughter of Gustav and Alma Mahler.

Schoenberg

Arnold Schoenberg gratefully bade farewell to his appendix after surgery here in Novemember 1925.

Webern

In 1932 Webern was admitted here after a number of fainting episodes while conducting rehearsals. No organic disease was found after a week of tests, and it was concluded that Webern, whose psychological health was never robust, was suffering from "nervous depression".

19 III Rennweg 91

Pfarrkirche Maria Geburt (Orphanage Church)

Mozart

This church was built in 1768 to serve the large adjacent orphanage. At its consecration in December 1768 the 12-year-old Mozart conducted his first complete setting of the Mass, the *Waissenhausmesse* (K139) and two smaller works. The Empress Maria Theresa was present.

A newspaper review noted that the music received "applause and admiration and Mozart conducted with great accuracy". But it was scant consolation for Mozart who had failed to overcome theatrical intrigues, which had prevented a production of *La Finta Semplice* during this visit (see V: 1A).

20 III Jacquingasse 8

Richard Strauss

To mark his 60th birthday the Austrian government gave to Richard Strauss a plot of land in the gardens of the Belvedere Palace on which he was invited to build a house (at his own expense). In return he would give to the Austrian National Library the original score of *Der Rosenkavalier*. The lease would lapse after 24 years.

After spending a small fortune on architects and builders Strauss was not pleased when he was informed that the "price" had been increased to include the scores of *Die Ägyptische Helena* and his ballet *Schlagobers* and, in addition, he must make a commitment to conduct 100 performances at the Staatsoper without fee in the following five years.

The building today houses the Embassy of the Netherlands.

21 Belvedere Palace Caretaker's Cottage

Bruckner

In the summer of 1895 Bruckner was finding the stairs to his apartment in the Hessgasse (see XII: 15) increasingly difficult to negotiate as his health declined. He was granted a "grace and favour" apartment in the Kustodientract alongside the Belvedere Palace.

Here Bruckner was able to enjoy walks in the superb gardens of the Palace. He received courtesy calls here from Hugo Wolf, Dvořák and Grieg.

Bruckner was composing his ninth symphony, which was to remain unfinished. He was working on the finale on the day of his death. There are over two hundred pages of sketches, which make clear that the fourth movement would have been a mighty finale. Whether or not Bruckner sanctioned the use of his *Te Deum* as a substitute for the unfinished finale is a matter that has taxed Bruckner scholars ever since.

The plaque commemorates Bruckner's death here on October 11th 1896.

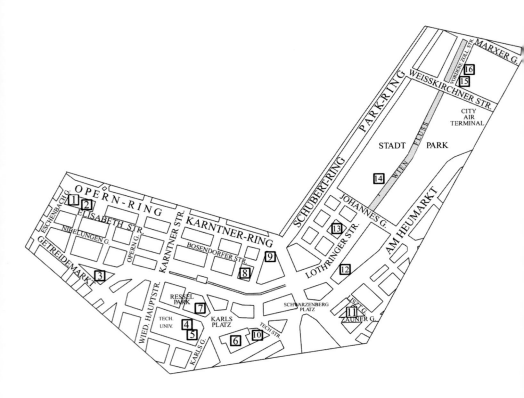

1 I Opernring 23

Suppé

Franz von Suppé moved into this spacious and well-appointed apartment in 1887. Here he composed his last operetta *Das Modell.*

Suppé's last years were marred by personal tragedy and ill-health. The death of his son Peter in 1891 was a devastating blow with which he found impossible to come to terms. He subsequently developed stomach cancer which was as painful as it was aggressive. His final weeks were particularly harrowing; unable to eat he became a living skeleton. At night, bizarrely, he began to sleep in a coffin. He died in 1895 at the age of 76.

2 I Elizabeth Strasse 16

Stolz

Robert Stolz lived in this apartment for over forty years, interrupted only by a period of self-imposed exile during the Second World War when he moved to the United States. He returned to Vienna in 1946 and reclaimed his apartment from the occupying Soviet officers who were living there.

Stolz was an integral part of the so-called "Silver Age of Operetta" in Vienna, the most distinguished member of which was Franz Lehár. He composed one opera in 1920 and then devoted himself entirely to operetta, composing over sixty. Although manifestly less gifted than Lehár, Stolz achieved great success, not only in Vienna but world-wide. He also composed film music for which he received two Oscar nominations.

After his death in 1975 at the age of 95 his coffin lay in state in the foyer of the Staatsoper as thousands paid their last respects.

3 I Friedrichstrasse 12

Sezession (Secession)

Mahler

In 1897 a group of artists led by Gustav Klimt "seceded" from the establishment's "Guild of Artists" which was based in the Künstlerhaus. A year later they built their own headquarters with its characteristic golden ball of laurel leaves surmounting the roof (dubbed by the Viennese "The Golden Cabbagehead").

In 1902 the sculptor Max Klinger unveiled his controversial statue of Beethoven in the room in which Klimt had painted his equally controversial Beethoven frieze. Mahler, who was by now the step-son-in-law of a founding member of the secessionists, Karl Moll, was asked to conduct a Beethoven concert at the official opening.

Plans to perform Beethoven's "Choral Symphony" with the Opera Chorus and the Vienna Philharmonic Orchestra were abandoned when the orchestra claimed that it was "overworked" by Mahler's incessant demands for rehearsals. He therefore made an arrangement of part of the "Ode to Joy" chorus for brass which he conducted at the opening.

Webern

In October 1924 Webern conducted the première of his "Five Sacred Songs" (Op 15) with members of the State Opera here.

4   Technische Hochschule (Technical University)

Johann (son) and Josef Strauss

A small plaque notes that both brothers were students here. Johann enrolled in 1841 at the behest of his famous father who insisted that his eldest son should have a secure job, which music did not provide. Johann studied book-keeping and accountancy with a view to becoming a bank clerk. But he was a most reluctant student and was eventually expelled after two years on a charge of "indiscipline".

In contrast, his brother Josef was a model student. He read engineering and architecture, qualifying in 1846. He subsequently designed a mechanical roadsweeper which saw service in Vienna. A reluctant musician, he agreed to conduct the Strauss Orchestra only after his elder brother had collapsed through exhaustion.

Vivaldi

Another plaque nearby records that this was the site of the former Spitaller Gottesacker Cemetery, which was abandoned in 1783. (The Technical University was built in 1818).

In this cemetery Vivaldi was buried in an unmarked grave in 1741.

5 IV Karlskirche

Bruckner

In October 1896 this wonderful Baroque Church was thronged by the great and good of Vienna for the funeral of Anton Bruckner. The Adagio of the Symphony No 7 in arrangement for wind band was played.

Brahms, the leading composer in Vienna at the time, arrived at the door of the church but did not enter. Muttering to an attendant "soon my coffin", he turned on his heel and went home. Brahms was already terminally ill and his aversion to Bruckner's music was well-known.

Hugo Wolf, who was such a staunch supporter of Bruckner, did not have a ticket and was refused admission.

Mahler

Gustav Mahler married Alma Schindler in the sacristy of the Karlskirche in March 1902. As director of the Hofoper Mahler had a high profile in Vienna, and to avoid undue attention he let it be known that the wedding would take place to 5.30pm. The large crowd who converged on the church were then informed that the ceremony had taken place at 1.30pm.

Mahler wore casual clothes and a slouch hat for his marriage to Alma, who was already in her fourth month of pregnancy. Mahler was 41, Alma 22.

Johann Strauss (son)

Six months after the death of his first wife Jetty, Strauss embarked upon a disastrous second marriage with Angelika (Lili) Dittrich. The marriage took place in the Karlskirche in May 1878.

The marriage did not last long; Lili began an affair with the director of the Theater an der Wien and eventually moved in with him.

6 Gluck monument

Alongside the Karlskirche is a statue of Gluck who lived in the nearby Wiedner Hauptstrasse (see IX : 9).

7 Brahms monument

The marble monument by Josef Weyr was unveiled in the Karlsplatz in 1908.

8 Karlsplatz / Bösendorferstrasse

Musikverein

The building of the Society of Friends of Music is described in chapter XXI.

9 I Kärntner Ring 16

Hotel Imperial

The Hotel Imperial was built as part of the Ringstrasse redevelopment in the late 1860s. It has been the favoured hotel of visiting Kings, Queens and Presidents ever since, although none of these worthies has merited a commemorative plaque; that honour belongs to **Wagner**.

In November 1875 Wagner stayed here in a suite of seven sumptuously appointed rooms, to which he felt entitled. He was in Vienna to supervise performances at the Hofoper of *Tannhäuser* and *Lohengrin*. Although Wagner's attitude to Vienna was always one of suspicion he must have been gratified by his reception on this occasion.

Hugo Wolf, whose worship for Wagner verged on idolatrous, managed to inveigle himself into the hotel and eventually succeeded in meeting Wagner. Wagner was amused by the fervour of Wolf, who was then a 15-year-old student at the Vienna Conservatory, and was gentle in his refusal to study Wolf's youthful piano scores.

10   IV Technikerstrasse 9

Schubert

In the shadow of the Karlskirche stood the "Fruhwirthhaus" in which Schubert rented a second floor apartment from February 1825 until the middle of 1826. In this low rambling house with its picturesque courtyard Schubert composed his String Quartet in D minor, settings of Goethe's *Wilhelm Meister* and Sir Walter Scott's "Lady of the Lake". His friend Moritz von Schwind lived with his family in the "Moonshine House" next door.

11   III Zaunergasse 1-3

Arnold Schoenberg Center

This superb institution was opened in March 1998 in the former Palais Fanto. The Arnold Schoenberg Center was founded by the City of Vienna and the Arnold Schoenberg Gesellschaft. The University of Southern California, where Schoenberg taught for many years, transferred its entire collection of papers, manuscripts and photographs relating to Schoenberg, and also the composer's library.

The Institution is a centre for research, exhibitions, publications, and the promotion of knowledge of Schoenberg's music and teaching.

It is a project of which Schoenberg would have wholeheartedly approved.

12   III Lothringerstrasse 18 – 20

Konzerthaus

(see XXI : B)

13   Beethoven Platz

Beethoven Monument

This memorial is by Kaspar von Zambusch and dates from 1880.

14   Parkring

Stadtpark

The Stadtpark was opened in 1862 on either bank of the River Wien. In the park are found statues of **Schubert, Bruckner** and **Stolz**. The famous memorial to **Johann Strauss (son)** has pride of place here.

The Stadtpark was a favourite place of **Brahms,** who lived nearby. He was a regular stroller in the park and often enjoyed a late-night coffee in one of the restaurants.

Before Emperor Franz Josef opened the Stadtpark to the public the so-called "Water Glacis" was here, a favourite haunt of army officers and minor nobility.

In 1843 **Johann Strauss (father)** introduced his finest waltz *Loreley Rhein Klänge* here.

On a sultry August evening in 1848 Strauss conducted the first performance of his "Radetzky March", which had to be repeated three times. Strauss clearly had a flair for the dramatic effect; a large picture of Field Marshall Radetzky was suddenly illuminated by torches as the march was played.

15   III Vordere Zollamtstrasse 13

Wiener Bürgertheater

Here stood the Wiener Bürgertheater, built in 1905 with 1130 seats. Many operettas of **Edmund Eysler** were first performed in this theatre.

16   III Vordere Zollamtstrasse 11

Berg

Berg lived with his parents in the house which stood here from 1908 until 1911, when he left home after his marriage to Helene Nahowski. Here he composed *Vier Lieder* (Op2) and the String Quartet (Op 3), a work which has an intensity which reflects his feelings for his future wife.

IX Wieden

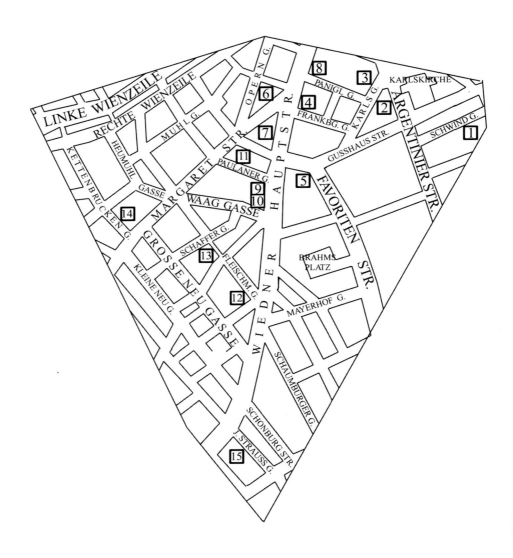

1   IV Schwindgasse 3

Wolf

In May 1896 Hugo Wolf moved into an apartment here which had been furnished by his friends. It was the first time in his life that he had a home to call his own.

Here he revised the score of his opera *Der Corregidor* and composed settings of poems by Byron and sonnets by Michelangelo.

He began work on a second opera, *Manuel Venegas*, but after completing fifty pages in short score he was overwhelmed by the effects of tertiary syphilis. He announced that he was the new director of the Court Opera, a post that had just been awarded to Mahler.

Wolf was exhibiting the classic signs of neurosyphilis, including dementia, violent behaviour and delusions. In September 1897 he was admitted to an asylum.

2   IV Argentiner Strasse 4 - 6

Szmanowski

On the fiftieth anniversary of the death of Karl Szmanowski a plaque was affixed to this house where the Polish composer lived from 1911 until 1914. An inveterate traveller, Szmanowski's stay here was interrupted by visits to Sicily and North Africa. His absorption by the ancient, Arabic and oriental cultures that he encountered coloured much of his music. He was in Vienna in the vain hope that his one-act opera *Hagith* would be given its première in the Austrian capital.

3   IV Karlsgasse 4

Brahms

At the beginning of 1872 Brahms rented two rooms on the third floor of this house. Later he acquired a third room to accommodate his expanding library, a valuable collection of first editions, engravings and manuscripts, which included such treasures as the original score

---

of Mozart's Symphony No. 40 in G minor. Here Brahms lived for 25 years until his death in 1897. Wealthy though Brahms became, the rooms changed very little during his tenancy.

His friends the Fellingers (see VII: 9) arranged for electric lighting to be installed, but this was the only significant change over a quarter of a century.

When the lady owner of the house died in 1886 Brahms found himself without a housekeeper, a crisis for the composer whose domestic skills were negligible. Frau Fellinger arranged for Frau Celestine Truxa, a widow with two children, to move into an adjacent apartment to look after Brahms. She discharged her responsibility faithfully until the composer's death.

Here Brahms received his visitors, including Hugo Wolf who approached Brahms for advice. Brahms received Wolf cordially and advised him to take lessons in counterpoint. For some reason Wolf took umbrage and began his vitriolic campaign against Brahms, notably in the periodical Salonblatt of which Wolf became editor.

In 1905 the building was demolished to make way for a controversial extension of the Technical University. It is a matter of regret that these historic rooms, in which the leading composer of the day in Vienna lived for 25 years, should have been sacrificed in this way. A commemorative plaque marks the site.

| 4 | **IV Frankenberggasse 6** |

Enescu

The Romanian-born violinist, composer and renowned teacher Georg Enescu lived in this house with his parents as a student. He was accepted by the Vienna Conservatory at the age of seven; already an accomplished violinist, Enescu had ambitions as a composer. He graduated with distinction before his eleventh birthday.

Enescu was a remarkable but vastly underrated composer. His opera "Oedipus" is a masterpiece.

5   IV Favoriten Strasse 8

Johann Strauss Theatre

Here stood the Johann Strauss Theatre, a beautiful building in the Baroque style which opened in 1908 seating 1200.

Many operas of Emmerich Kálmán received first performances here including his greatest work *Die Csárdásfürstin* in 1915. Another member of the "Silver Age of Operetta", Robert Stolz, also had operettas premièred here including *Der Tanz ins Glück* and *Eine Sommernacht,* both in 1921. Lehár's *Paganini* also received its first performance in 1925 in this theatre.

6   IV Wiedner Hauptstrasse 10/Margaretenstrasse 10-16

Freihaus Theatre

Mozart

A mosaic on a building at the western end of the triangular plot bounded by the Wiedner Haupstrasse, Margaretenstrasse and Operngasse marks the site of the Freihaus. This huge complex of courtyards and tenement buildings included over 300 apartments, a tavern, a church, a summer pavilion and a rather run-down theatre, the "Theater auf der Wieden". This theatre was managed by Emmanuel Schikaneder, a friend of Mozart and a fellow Freemason.

In this theatre Mozart directed the first performance of *Die Zauberflöte* in September 1791, a few weeks before his death. Schikaneder provided the libretto.

The summer pavilion, much restored, in which Mozart occasionally composed parts of the opera is today on view in the garden of the Mozarteum in Salzburg.

The Freihaus became increasingly decrepit and was pulled down in the nineteenth century.

7   IV Margaretenstrasse 7

Mahler

Here stood the house in which Gustav Mahler occupied an apartment on the fourth floor while he was a student at the Vienna Conservatory. He lived here from 1887-8 when he was 17. He financed his studies by giving piano lessons.

8 IV Wiedner Hauptstrasse 7

Dvořák

Dvořák stayed at the former hotel "The Golden Lamb" on his visits to Vienna to see his friend and mentor Brahms. The latter made strenuous efforts to persuade Dvořák to move to Vienna on a permanent basis, even putting his own fortune at the disposal of the Czech composer. But Dvořák would not leave Prague.

9 IV Wiedner Hauptstrasse 32

Gluck

Christoph Willibald von Gluck moved into this fine house "Zum silbernen Löwen" after an advantageous marriage to the daughter of a wealthy merchant in 1752.

Between 1774 and 1779 he devoted all his operatic output to Paris until he tired of the intrigues at the Paris opera and retired to a luxurious life-style in this house. Dinner guests who enjoyed Gluck's hospitality here included Mozart and his wife Constanza in 1783.

Gluck's death came in 1787 at the age of 73 after he ignored the advice of his doctor and overindulged in fine wine once too often.

Schubert

In 1825 the artist Wilhelm Rieder, a close friend of Schubert, lived in this house. His watercolour portrait of Schubert, dating from this year, is believed to represent the best likeness of the composer.

Schubert lived close by in the Technikerstrasse (see VIII: 10) and did not possess a piano. He persuaded Rieder, who also had musical inclinations, to purchase a fine square piano which Schubert could use. He felt that he would be inspired by the ambiance of the "Gluck-Haus".

10   IV Wiedner Hauptstrasse 36

Sibelius

In 1890 Sibelius arrived in Vienna armed with a letter of introduction to Brahms furnished by Busoni. Brahms no longer gave lessons and Sibelius sought out Karl Goldmark and Robert Fuchs for tuition in composition.

Sibelius seems to have been something of a party-animal in those days, living wildly beyond his means and often carousing into the small hours.

An audition with the Vienna Philharmonic Orchestra as a violinist was unsuccessful because the Finn was deemed to suffer from "nerves".

Here he set poems by Runeberg and began work on the "Kullervo Symphony".

11   IV Paulanergasse 12

Kálmán

After Lehár, Emmerich Kálmán was, perhaps, the most gifted composer of the "Silver Age of Operetta".

In 1909 he moved into a three-roomed apartment in this house with Paula Dworczak, a lady with whom he lived for seventeen years but never married. Here he composed *Die Urlauber.*

12   IV Fleischmanngasse 1

Lortzing

Albert Lortzing was the leading German composer of comic opera of the nineteenth century. In 1846 he moved to this house after his appointment as Kapellmeister at the Theater an der Wien (see XX). Here he completed his opera *Der Waffenschmied* which was given at the theatre in 1846. The following year he composed *Zum Grossadmiral* in this house.

In 1848 he composed *Regina* which proved to be his undoing; the libretto was considered too subversive in those revolutionary days and he was obliged to resign his post.

13 IV Kleinschmidgasse 1

Suppé

In 1882 Suppé resigned from the musical directorship of the Carltheater (see VI: 23) where he had enjoyed so much success. He moved to an apartment in this tiny street where he lived for a year while working on his opera *Die Afrikareise*. This work, like most of his subsequent operas, was a failure.

14 IV Kettenbrückengasse 6

Schubert

In September 1828 Schubert's health declined, probably because of the onset of tertiary syphilis, the disease that he had contracted five years previously. His doctor advised him to leave the city centre for the cleaner air of the suburbs. Thus Schubert lived for the last three months of his life in this house as a guest of his brother Ferdinand and his wife.

This attractive Biedermeier house was of recent construction and had not yet fully dried out; furthermore the sanitation facilities were of a rudimentary standard which may well have been a contribution to Schubert's early death. Schubert occupied a room on the first floor overlooking the street. The apartment is preserved as a museum.

Although not well, Schubert composed some of his greatest music at this time, including the great String Quintet in C major.

At the end of October 1828 Schubert became very ill indeed, probably from a typhoid infection. He wrote to his friend Schober requesting novels by James Fennimore Cooper. On November 19th 1828 after days of intermittent delirium he said solemnly "Here is my end", turned to the wall and died. He was 31.

During his visit to Vienna in 1838-9 Schumann paid a courtesy call on Ferdinand Schubert here. In a pile of papers left by the dead composer Schumann discovered, the score of Schubert's Symphony No. 9 in C major (The Great).

15   IV Johann Strauss Gasse 4

Johann Strauss (son)

In 1875 Strauss purchased two adjoining plots of land in the Igelgasse. The street was renamed in 1900, the year after the composer's death. His first wife Jetty supervised the construction of a palatial and elegant town house on the land, a fitting residence for the wealthy and famous composer. Unfortunately Jetty died in 1878 as the house was nearing completion. Strauss moved in with his second wife Lili. After this disastrous marriage ended in divorce Strauss shared the house with his third wife Adèle until his death in 1899.

The accommodation comprised a dining room, study and billiard room on the ground floor and a salon and several bedrooms upstairs. The decorations were expensive with many works of art on display.

Towards the end of his life Strauss became increasingly reclusive, spending hours in his billiard room, which he called his "coffee house".

Brahms was a frequent guest here; other visitors included Bruckner, Puccini and Goldmark.

In 1944 the house was destroyed during a bombing raid. A commemorative plaque marks the site.

X Mariahilf and Margareten

1   **VI Mariahilf Church**

Haydn

A life-sized statue of Josef Haydn was erected in front of the church in 1887.

2   **VI Windmühlgasse 18**

Johann Strauss (father) and Lanner

In 1819 Josef Lanner formed a string trio which played dance music in local taverns. Lanner invited the 15-year-old Strauss to join the group as a viola player. They became firm friends; contrary to popular opinion in Vienna the friendship survived their professional separation, after which they led their own rival orchestras.

For a while they shared lodgings in this house. The impecunious pair also shared food, clothes and girl-friends.

3   **VI Theobaldgasse 16**

Lehár

Franz Lehár lived in this house from 1919 until 1931. He divided his time between here and his villa at Bad Ischl. During this period Lehár became associated with the tenor Richard Tauber. His most successful works during his time here were *Der Zarewitsch* and *Das Land des Lächelns* ("The Land of Smiles").

4   **Theater an der Wien**

See XX

5   **VI Laimgrubengasse 22**

Beethoven

Beethoven lived on the first floor of this house between November 1822 and May 1823. The rooms are now preserved as a museum.

During his stay here he was working on the *Missa Solemnis* and the Choral Symphony. He also composed his last Piano Sonata (Op111) and completed the overture "The Consecration of the House" here.

In April 1823 Beethoven received a visit from the 11-year-old Franz Liszt who was about to make his Viennese début in the Redoutensaal. After Liszt had played one of J.S. Bach's 48 Preludes and Fugues., Beethoven asked the boy if he could transpose the fugue into another key of Beethoven's choosing. Listz immediately did so and received a kiss on the forehead from Beethoven.

Liszt related this account to a pupil over fifty years later, placing the episode in the "Schwarzpanierhaus", Beethoven's last residence. As Beethoven did not move to the "Schwarzpanierhaus" until 1825 Liszt's memory had deceived him. Successive biographers of Beethoven and Liszt have failed to realise the error.

6   VI Gumpendorferstrasse 11 - 13

Café Sperl

The legendary Café Sperl is the quintessential Viennese coffeehouse, although much modified since its opening in 1880. Among its distinguished clientèle were **Lehár** and **Kálmán**, who lived nearby, and also **Brahms**.

7   VI Gumpendorferstrasse 17

Millöcker

A commemorative plaque marks the site of the house in which Karl Millöcker, the composer of operettas, was born in 1842.

8   VI Gumpendorferstrasse 47

Lanner

Josef Lanner lived here between 1832 and 1838.

9   V Schönbrunnerstrasse 52 – Josef Kirche

Schubert

On November 21st 1828, a rainy Friday afternoon, Schubert's coffin was carried to this church for his funeral service. Here the choir sang Schubert's *Pax Vobiscum* (D551) to words set by his friend Schober for the occasion, followed by a funeral motet by Gänsbacher. The coffin was then taken to the church of St Lorenz and St Gertrud in Währing for a second blessing (see XIII : 4)

10 St Ägyd Church

Haydn

The funeral service of Josef Haydn was held in this church on June 1st 1809. Vienna was occupied by the French and the funeral passed almost unnoticed. The following day a Requiem Mass by Haydn's younger brother Michael, who had predeceased him by three years, was sung here.

Schubert

In 1813 Schubert's father married Anna Kleyenbock here, just under a year after the death of Schubert's mother. It is not known whether Schubert, who was in his last year at school, attended the ceremony. Anna would show great kindness to her stepson and Schubert was very fond of her.

11 VI Haydngasse 19

Haydn

In 1793, after an artistically and financially successful visit to England, Haydn purchased this house. At that time it was a single-storey building in what was then the Kleine Steingasse. A second visit to England accrued more funds and Haydn commissioned the rebuilding of the house with a second storey.

At the end of 1796 Haydn moved in with his wife, his niece, a cook and his secretary and music-copyist Johann Elssler (the father of the famous dancer Fanny Elssler).

Haydn's marriage to his wife Anna had been an unhappy one and the couple were estranged for most of the 40 year marriage. In 1800, with her arthritis causing increasing incapacity, Haydn sent her to Baden, where she died.

In this house Haydn composed his great oratorios "Creation" and "The Seasons". Visitors here included Constanza Mozart and the composers Cherubini and Weber.

During the French invasion in May 1809 the elderly Haydn and his staff were badly shaken by a stray cannon ball which landed near the house. Although by now very weak, Haydn continued to play the Austrian National Anthem (his composition) in gentle defiance of the French invaders. He became increasingly frail; when Napoleon Bonaparte heard about his condition he personally ordered a Guard of Honour to be mounted outside the house.

Haydn died here on May 31st 1809. The house is now the Haydn Museum. In one wing are housed the Brahms memorial rooms with items of furniture, taken from Brahms's last residence in the Karlsgasse (see VIII : 3) together with other mementos of the composer.

Brahms had no connection with this house and it is a disappointing memorial.

12 Westbahnhof

Mahler

Early on a cold December morning in 1907 some 200 people gathered on a platform to give a surprise farewell send-off to Gustav Mahler and his wife Alma who were leaving Vienna for New York. Mahler had been virtually hounded out of Vienna by an anti-Semitic press and by enemies Mahler had made in his ruthless drive for perfection at the Hofoper.

The gathering had been organised by Anton von Weber *et al.* Among those present were Schoenberg, Berg, Zemlinsky and the artist Gustav Klimt, the founder of the Secessionist movement with which Mahler had been closely associated. An astonished Mahler arrived to find his carriage compartment bedecked with flowers.

It was a sombre and emotional occasion; all those present realised that they were witnessing not only the end of Mahler's tenure in Vienna but also the end of an era.

13   XII Wallgasse 18 - 20

Raimund Theater

Opened as the Mariahilfer Burgtheater in 1893 this theatre seats 1200. A bust of Robert Stolz in the foyer recognises the importance of this theatre in the world of operetta. A number of Stolz's works received their first performances here, including *Das Glücksmädel* (1910), *Die eiserne Jungfrau* (1911) and *Die Liebe geht um* (1922).

14   Gaudenzdorfer Gürtel

Haydn Park

In 1809 Haydn was buried in what was then the Hundsthurmer Friedhof. Three days later the grave was desecrated by supporters of Professor Gall's "skull theory", and the head was removed (see IV : 20).

When Prince Esterhazy ordered the exhumation of Haydn's remains prior to reburial at Eisenstadt the grave digger found only the torso and Haydn's wig.

In 1926 the cemetery was deconsecrated and made into a public park. Haydn's gravestone (erected in 1814) was incorporated into a memorial.

XI Neubau and Josefstadt

1   VIII Zieglergasse 15

Site of the Apollo Ballroom

The Apollosaal opened its doors for the first time in 1808. On that first night this remarkable establishment admitted 4000 people: **Hummel** composed Twelve Minuets and Trios (Op 27) for the occasion.

There was a very large ballroom with the orchestra placed in a balcony above. The huge circular dining room was furnished with a hundred tables. There were also over forty public rooms, fountains waterfalls and even a lake complete with swans.

Among the conductors was **Josef Lanner. Johann Strauss (father)** performed here often, composing his *Apollo-Waltzer* in honour of the establishment.

The Apollo was comparatively short-lived; it was almost inevitable that such extravagancies would lead to bankruptcy, which occurred in 1819. After that, with a new owner, the Apollosaal went into decline. It closed in 1839 and became a rather mundane soap and candle factory. It was destroyed by fire and the ruin pulled down in 1876.

2   VIII Westbahnstrasse 2 - 4

Ziehrer

The operetta composer Carl Michael Ziehrer was born in this house in May 1843.

3   VII Siebensterngasse 19

Café Schoner

This venerable restaurant was the haunt of **Johann Strauss (son)** and **Franz Lehàr. Alban Berg** who lived nearby (see next entry), was also often seen here.

VII Schweighofergasse 8

Berg

When the family home in the Tuchlauben (see IV: 8), in which Berg had been born, was scheduled for demolition, the family moved to a large apartment in the house which stood here. The Bergs lived here from 1899 until 1905.

The period that he lived here was not uneventful. In 1900 Berg's father died suddenly, an event which caused the family financial difficulties, at least in the short term. Berg was then 15.

In 1903, after taking his final matriculation examination Berg made a half-hearted attempt at suicide. (He passed the examination at the second time of asking).

A brief affair with a local girl in Carinthia ended when the girl became pregnant. Presumably money changed hands and the episode was smoothed over.

There was an unexpected sequel many years later. Forty years after Berg's death his widow Helene, then 90, met the illegitimate daughter of her late husband. Berg's daughter, herself nearly 70, had no knowledge or interest in her father's musical achievements.

5 **VII Kirchberggasse 17**

Goldmark

Karl Goldmark lived in this apartment house in the first half of the nineteenth century.

6 **St. Ulrichs Platz – St Ulrich's Church**

In this eighteenth century church both **Josef Lanner** and **Johann Strauss (son)** were baptised. In 1752 **Gluck** married the daughter of a wealthy merchant here.

For some years **Schubert's** brother Ferdinand was associated with the church. In September 1825 Ferdinand directed a performance here of his brother's Mass in C Major (D452) together with some of Schubert's smaller liturgical works.

Three years later, a week after Schubert's death, friends and admirers of the dead composer were invited to a sung Requiem Mass in memory of Schubert. The mass chosen was Mozart's Requeim.

7   VII Mechitaristen gasse 5

Lanner

Josef Lanner was born in this house in April 1801. His father was a glove maker.

8   VII Lerchenfelder Strasse 15

Johann Strauss (father and son)

A commemorative plaque marks the site of the house called "Zur goldenen Eule" (The Golden Owl). In July 1825 the newly-married Johann Strauss (father) and his wife Maria Anna, already pregnant, moved into a small apartment in this house. Three months later their first child, a son also named Johann, was born here.

By 1890 the building was so run-down that it was demolished, an event witnessed by Johann Strauss (son).

9   VII Lerchenfelder Strasse 65

Mozart

At the end of July 1783 Mozart took his wife Constanza to Salzburg for a potentially difficult meeting with his father who had disapproved strongly of the marriage. They left their 6-week-old baby son Raimund with a wet-nurse at the house which then stood on this site. In August the baby died of "intestinal cramps". It is thought unlikely that the Mozarts found out until they returned to Vienna in November.

10   Altlerchenfelder Church

Schubert

The present building, completed in 1861, was constructed on the foundations of a church dating from the eighteenth century. In this former church **Schubert's** brother, Ferdinand was choirmaster from 1820 until 1824.

For Palm Sunday 1820 Schubert composed his Six Antiphons (D696) for the church. A week later Schubert was to direct the first performance of his oratorio Lazarus, but the work was unfinished (and would remain so to the regret of all Schubertians). In its place Schubert conducted a performance of Haydn's "Nelson Mass".

Ferdinand directed the first performance of his brother's Mass in A♭ in 1823 in this church.

|11|　XVI Thalia Strasse 1

Wagner

Here stood the Thalia Theatre. Of wooden construction it seated 3000 and was used only in summer. In 1857 Wagner's *Tannhäuser* received its first Viennese performance before a full house here.

|12|　XVI Neulerchenfelder Strasse 14

Johann Strauss (son)

At the inn "The Blue Bottle" which stood here Johann Strauss (son) introduced his *Liguoriana-Seufzer, Scherz-Polka* in1848.

|13|　VII Josefstädter Strasse 57

Beethoven

Beethoven lived in the house "Zu den zwei Wachsstöcken", which used to stand here, in 1820. He was much preoccupied with the composition of the *Missa Solemnis* to celebrate the appointment of his patron Archduke Rudolf who was to be ordained Bishop of Olmütz. Such was the scale of his work that it would not be completed until three years after the ordination.

Beethoven's other problem at this time was the continuing litigation with regard to the guardianship of his nephew Karl.

14   Theater in der Josefstadt

This old theatre opened in 1788 as a variety theatre. After a major renovation in 1822 it reopened with a gala concert at which **Beethoven** conducted his "Consecration of the House" overture, specially commissioned for the occasion. It was probably the last time that Beethoven conducted in public; because of increasing deafness he was unable to hear soft passages and frequently lost control of the orchestra.

In 1834 **Conradin Kreutzer's** opera *Dar Nachtlager in Granada* was given its first performance here.

In 1840 **Franz von Suppé** was appointed (unpaid) third conductor here. He composed incidental music to plays staged here including "Morning, Noon and Night in Vienna" in 1884.

In his early days with his new orchestra **Johann Strauss (son)** often performed in this theatre.

Today the theatre is used only for the performance of plays.

15   VII Zeltgasse 14

Eysler

The plaque on this house commemorates the death here in 1949 of Edmund Eysler. He composed two operas and over fifty operettas which, although very popular in their day they have gradually disappeared from the repertory.

16   VII Piaristengasse 32

Wolf

In this attractive house known as "Zum schwarzen Lamm", Hugo Wolf lived in 1896. Although unwell from the effects of secondary syphilis he composed his opera *Der Corregidor.*

17   Piaristenkirche Maria Treu

This splendid church was completed in 1753, although the twin towers were added a hundred years later.

On Good Friday 1771 **Josef Haydn** conducted his *Stabat Mater* here with a large orchestra and chorus before a huge congregation.

In June 1791 **Mozart** walked in the Corpus Christi procession which set out from and returned to this church. Four months later he attended Mass here and lunched with the priests. Apparently he wished his son Karl to be accepted as a pupil at the Piarist Seminary.

Suppé conducted the first performance of his Requiem here in 1855. It had been written in memory of the theatre impresario Franz Pokorny.

In November 1861 **Bruckner** was examined on the organ, the final examination for the diploma of the Vienna Conservatoire. It would enable Bruckner to teach harmony and counterpoint in music schools. The story is well known; the examiners included **Simon Sechter** and the conductor **Johann Herbeck**. Bruckner was given an eight-bar theme on which to improvise. After the conclusion of Bruckner's performance the examiners sat spellbound in admiration to which Herbeck gave voice: "He should have been testing us."

18   VII Florianigasse 8a

Schweitzer

In this small house Albert Schweitzer lived in 1909. Born in 1875 Schweitzer was a philosopher, theologian, doctor, missionary and a fine organist. (He was a pupil of Widor). He was also one of the leading authorities on J.S.Bach.

19   Rathaus

The neo-Gothic Town Hall was modelled on the Town Hall of Brussels. It was completed in 1883. For the first "City Ball" in 1890 **Johann Strauss (son)** performed his newly composed *Rathaus – Ball – Tänze* and **Ziehrer** his *Weiner Bürger*.

In the beautiful arched courtyard, where **Stolz's** singspiel *Der liebe Augustin* received its première in 1953, summer concerts are held.

The Wiener Stadtbibliothek housed here includes a rich collection of musical scores including many by Schubert.

20   I Bartensteingasse 3

Mahler

Gustav Mahler lived in this apartment building from 1877-8. He moved in just before taking up the post of Director of the Hofoper.

In September 1897 Hugo Wolf knocked on the door. Mahler was out and Wolf informed the housekeeper who opened the door that he, Wolf, was now the Director of the Opera. The housekeeper, startled and not a little alarmed, slammed the door shut. Wolf, in the throes of neurosyphilis was admitted to an asylum shortly after this incident.

21   I Reichsratstrasse 9

Eduard Strauss

In this imposing residence Eduard Strauss died in 1916. He was the youngest of the three sons of Strauss (father), and the least gifted. Nevertheless he was an accomplished violinist and conducted the Strauss orchestra until he disbanded it in 1901.

22   Auersperg Palace

This palace, constructed early in the eighteenth century has been much modified both internally and externally.

Late in the eighteenth century both **Gluck** and **Dittersdorf** were engaged to conduct performances here.

In 1762 the six-year-old **Mozart** and his sister were guests here. Many years later in 1786 Mozart directed amateur forces in a performance of *Idomeneo*. The theatre in the palace where this took place no longer exists.

23   VIII Auerspergstrasse 9

Schoenberg

Here stood the Auersperg Sanatorium where Schoenberg's first wife Mathilde died in 1923 from gall-bladder and liver problems. Schoenberg lived here for a time during her final illness.

24   VIII Trautsohngasse 2

Beethoven

Beethoven lived on the third floor of the "Fingerlingscher Haus" in 1819-20. Here he composed the Credo of the *Missa Solemnis*.

To his intense relief he was awarded custody of his nephew Karl while living here. It was a role for which he was hardly suited.

St Stephen's (Crucifix Chapel)

Deutschordenshaus

The former Bogner's Café

The Three Hatchets Inn

Ballgasse 4 (Beethoven)

The former Jahn's Café

Seilerstätte 30 (Nicolai)

The former Green Anchor Inn

Schulerstrasse 8 (Mozart)

Stadtkonvict (Schubert)

Old University

Schönlaterngasse 7a (Schumann)

Collalto Palace and Kirche Am Hof   *Tiefer Graben 18 (Mozart)*

Schottenkirche   *Pasqualati House (Beethoven)*

National Library and Redoutensaal

Hofburg Chapel

Augustiner Kirche

Lobkowitz Palace

Spiegelgasse 9 (Schubert)

Michaelerhaus (Haydn)

Obere Donaustrasse 5 (Schoenberg)

Augartensaal

Prater Strasse 54 (J.Strauss–son)

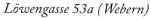

Löwengasse 53a (Webern)

Sofiensaal before the disastrous fire

Rasumovsky Palace (Beethoven)

Erdberg Strasse 17 (Schubert)

Ungargasse 5 (Beethoven)

Auernbruggergasse 2 (Mahler)

Pfarrkirche Maria Geburt (Mozart)

Belvedere Palace – caretaker's cottage (Bruckner)

Brahms Memorial

J. Strauss (son) memorial

Wiedner Hauptstrasse 7 (Dvořák)

Wiedner Hauptstrasse 32 (Gluck)   *Fleischmanngasse 1 (Lortzing)*

Kettenbruckengasse 6 (Schubert)   *Haydngasse 19 (Haydn)*

Laimgrubengasse 22 (Beethoven)

Original gravestone of Haydn

St Ulrich's Church

Mechitaristengasse 5 (Lanner)

Josefstadt Theatre

Trautsohngasse 2 (Beethoven)

*Left: Dreifaltigkeitkirche
(Beethoven, Schubert)*

*Above: Währinger Strasse 41
(Bruckner)*

Schubert Park (original graves of Beethoven and Schubert)

Nüssdorfer Strasse 54 (Schubert)

Säulengasse 3 (Schubert)

Volksoper

Lichtental Church (Schubert)   *Liechtenstein Strasse 68-70 (Schoenberg)*

Döblinger Haupstrasse 92
(Beethoven)

Grinzinger Friedhof
- Mahler's grave

Grinzinger Strasse 64 (Beethoven)

Pfarrplatz 2 (Beethoven)

Probusgasse 6 (Beethoven)

Beethoven Ruhe

Kahlenberger Strasse 26 (Beethoven) *Hackhofergasse 18 (Lehár)*

Xaipe Villa (Beethoven) *Hadikgasse 72 (Wagner)*

Trautmansdorfgasse 27 (Berg)

*Maxing Strasse 18
(J. Strauss – son)*

St Marx Cemetery entrance

Mozart's "grave"

Grave of Beethoven

Grave of Schubert

Grave of Brahms

Grave of Schoenberg

Baden Pfarrkirche (Mozart)

Rathausgasse 10, Baden
(Beethoven)

Dreimarktsteingasse 13 (J. Strauss – son)   *Jeneweingasse 17 (Beethoven)*

Theater an der Wien

Vienna State Opera

Musikverein

Konzerthaus

XII Hernals and Alsergrund

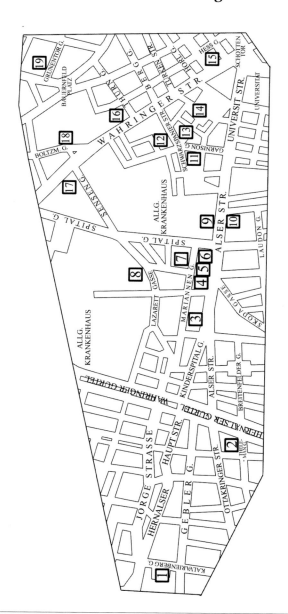

1   XVII Kalvarienbergkirche (St. Bartholomew's church)

Schubert

In this church on November 3rd 1828, two weeks before his death, Schubert attended a Latin Requiem Mass, which had been composed by his brother Ferdinand. After Schubert's death Ferdinand dedicated the work to the memory of his dead brother. It was probably the last music that Schubert heard.

2   XVII Thelemangasse 8

Eysler

A plaque commemorates the birth here in 1874 of Edmund Eysler.

3   IX Alser Strasse 30

Beethoven

Here stood the town palace of Count Karl Lichnowsky, a musical connoisseur and fine amateur pianist. This was Beethoven's first residence in Vienna after his arrival in 1792. He at first occupied an attic room, but before long Lichnowsky welcomed him into his home as a house guest, even putting a horse at his disposal.

Lichnowsky held concerts in his home on Friday mornings for which he hired professional musicians, notably the violinist Ignaz Schuppanzigh. It was on one of these occasions that Beethoven's Piano Trios, which he designated his Opus 1, were played for the first time. Beethoven lived here until 1795.

4   IX Alserstrasse 20

Brahms

A tablet above the door of the present building notes that this was the home of Theodor Billroth, the great nineteenth century surgeon and an excellent amateur musician. The house was demolished in 1906.

Billroth was a friend of Brahms and a number of the composer's works were heard for the first time in Billroth's richly decorated music room.

The Sextet for Strings in G, the Marienlieder, the Piano Trio in C major and the String Quintet in F major were played here, with Billroth playing either violin or viola.

5   IX Alserstrasse 18

Kálman

Emmerich Kálman left Budapest for Vienna in 1909 to supervise the production of his operetta *Ein Herbstmanöver* at the Theater an der Wien, a work which brought him instant success. He lived in a small apartment in a house which stood here.

6   IX Alserstrasse 8

Goldmark

Karl Goldmark lived in an apartment in a house, which used to occupy this site.

7   IX Mariannegasse 20

Mahler

In May 1911 Mahler, at the age of 50, was a dying man. A diseased heart valve had become infected, a condition known as sub-acute bacterial endocarditis. A physician in Paris suggested to his wife Alma that she might take the terminally ill composer to Vienna, the city in which he had found fulfilment, albeit briefly.

Thus Mahler was brought to the Löw Clinic here. The Viennese who had forced Mahler out of Vienna four years previously tried to make amends; hundreds of people stood outside the clinic, and Mahler's room was filled with flowers. Viennese newspapers carried daily medical bulletins on the condition of the composer.

Mahler's last year had been deeply unhappy. Unable to cope with her husband's driven personality, Alma had sought solace first in alcohol and then in the arms of the architect Walter Gropius. Mahler's anguish over the affair with Gropius is reflected in his tenth symphony on which he was working. The searing intensity of the music and the pleas to Alma scrawled on the manuscript are indications of his despair.

As his condition deteriorated, Mahler gave the sketches of the tenth symphony to Alma; tacit acknowledgement that he would be unable to complete the work.

Mahler died here on May 18th 1911.

The English musicologist Deryk Cooke made what he called a "performing version" of the tenth symphony. Cooke's innate modesty should not prevent recognition of his achievement, which was remarkable.

8   IX Lazarettgasse 14

Wolf

Here stood the Lower Austria Provincial Lunatic Asylum to which Hugo Wolf was committed (at his own request after attempting to drown himself) in 1898.

Wolf was displaying all the signs of neurosyphilus, the tertiary stage of the disease; inappropriate and sometimes violent behaviour, delusions and grossly exalted ideas of his position. A quarrel with Mahler over the staging of his opera *Der Corregidor* had precipitated the final phase.

Wolf spent the last four years and four months of his life here under the watchful eyes of the male nurses. He died in February 1903 just before his forty-third birthday. To the end of his days he received visits from his faithful lover Melanie Köchert, wife of the Imperial Jeweller (see V: 11).

9   **Allgemeines Krankenhaus – Vienna General Hospital**

In the autumn of 1823 **Antonio Salieri**, his mind deranged, attempted to commit suicide by cutting his throat. He was brought to this hospital and placed in secure accommodation in a ward known as "Fools Tower".

Rumours were soon circulating around Vienna that Salieri had confessed to poisoning Mozart, although evidence for this "confession" is lacking. When a former pupil, the pianist Ignaz Moscheles, visited Salieri the old man earnestly denied any involvement in the death of Mozart.

Salieri died after two years here at the age of 75. It was a sad and ignominious end to the life of a distinguished musician who had played a leading role in Viennese musical life for more than half a century.

In that same year 1825 the Bohemian composer and principal court organist **Jan Hugo Voříšek** died in this hospital from tuberculosis.

In 1823 **Schubert** was admitted to the hospital after a recurrence of the symptoms of secondary syphilis. He was in hospital for some weeks, no doubt being dosed with mercury, the only treatment available. His hair fell out and he wore a wig. While here he composed some songs for his song-cycle *Die Schöne Müllerin*.

10 Dreifaltigkeitkirche – Trinity Church

Beethoven

The funeral of Beethoven took place in this eighteenth-century church on March 29th 1827. It was a spectacular occasion. So great were the crowds that the cortège took ninety minutes to cover the 500 yards from Beethoven's home to the church. Among the pall-bearers were Hummel and Kreutzer; the torch-bearers included Schubert.

The music included a *Miserere*, set to two of Beethoven's *Equali* for trombone. A brass band played an arrangement of the funeral march of Beethoven's Piano Sonata in A$^\flat$ (Opus 26). The pressure from the enormous crowd was so great that many fainted and were taken across the road to the hospital. Soldiers from the nearby Alser barracks were called out to maintain order.

Schubert

In 1828 Schubert composed *Glaube, Hoffnung und Liebe* for the solemn consecration of a newly-founded bell for the church.

In 1829, nearly a year after Schubert's death, his brother Ferdinand conducted the first performance of the Mass in E^b Major (D950) in this church.

11   IX Garnisongasse 7

Beethoven

In the house which stood here, "Roter Haus", Beethoven lived for a few weeks in 1804 with his friend Stephan von Breuning until a quarrel ended the arrangement. Beethoven was occupied by early sketches for *Fidelio* and by Josephine von Deym who had just become a widow. The composer and Josephine became very close for a time.

12   IX Schwarzpanierstrasse 15

Beethoven

Beethoven's last residence, the "Schwarzpanierhaus", was demolished in 1903. The front door to Beethoven's apartment was rescued and is exhibited in the Beethoven Museum in the "Pasqualatihaus" (see IV: 32).

Beethoven moved into an apartment in the former Benedictine cloister in October 1825. Here he composed his last music, the late string quartets Op 131, 135 and a new finale for Op 130.

His health declined, his bowels being particularly troublesome. In the summer of 1826 came the most devastating blow of all; his nephew Karl attempted to commit suicide at Baden (see XVIII: A12). Karl recovered and was packed off into the army. Beethoven's health deteriorated rapidly. He developed pneumonia and pleurisy together with cirrhosis of the liver.

There are many accounts of the pain and misery of Beethoven's last weeks. Fluid in his abdomen was repeatedly drained directly on to the vermin-infested mattress. He was prescribed copious draughts of wine which may have exacerbated his condition. Research on Beethoven's hair has revealed an astonishingly high lead content.

The most likely explanation is the amount of wine that Beethoven consumed. The tart local wine was treated with a lead compound to make it more palatable.

Visitors included Schubert and Hummel. Beethoven's financial affairs became a problem and he was grateful and relieved to receive a gift of £100 from the Philharmonic Society of London.

The end came in suitably dramatic circumstances, described by Schubert's friend Anselm Hüttenbrenner, who was present.

During a violent thunderstorm on March 26th 1827 Beethoven, who had been in a coma, opened his eyes and raised his arm with fist clenched. His arm was lowered and he was dead. According to Hüttenbrenner, Beethoven's sister-in-law Johanna, with whom he had fought such a bitter and protracted battle for the custody of Karl, was also present. Her presence suggests the possibility of a deathbed reconciliation between them.

Three days later, the day of the funeral, a crowd estimated at up to 20,000 gathered in the square outside the house.

13 IX Ferstelgasse 6

Webern

In 1902 Anton won Webern's father, a mining engineer by profession, was promoted to a ministerial post and the family moved to an apartment in this house. For young Webern, now 18, it was conveniently close to the University at which he had enrolled to study music history and philosophy. He came under the tuition of Schoenberg in 1904 and his compositions at that time, string quartets and other chamber works reflect the influences of his teacher. He also composed his Passacaglia here which he nominated as his Opus 1.

14 Votivkirche

Wolf

In this mid-nineteenth century church with its twin filigree spires the funeral of Hugo Wolf took place in February 1903.

Although largely ignored while he was alive, Wolf drew a distinguished congregation for his funeral. Mahler was present together with many artists from the Hofoper. The young Webern was also there.

Music played during the service included a Wolf song for mixed choir and the Adagio from Bruckner's 9th Symphony.

15   I Hessgasse 7

Bruckner

Anton Bruckner moved into a fourth-floor apartment in this building in 1877. He lived here on a rent-free basis (the building was owned by an admirer) until 1895 when growing infirmity made climbing the stairs too difficult. He was then granted a "grace and favour" residence at Belvedere Palace by the Emperor (see VII: 21).

Virtually all of Bruckner's creative energy here was devoted to the Symphonies Nos. 6, 7 and 8. He began his ninth here but died before he was able to complete it.

Although the apartment was spacious it was furnished very simply. His one "luxury" was an English brass bed.

16   IX Währingerstrasse 26

Mozart

The small commemorative plaque over the door marks the site of the house "The Three Stars". Mozart and Constanza moved into an apartment facing the garden here in June 1788.

The plaque refers to *Così fan Tutte* although the composition of this opera is properly associated with Judenplatz 4 (see IV: 19).

Here Mozart composed his last three symphonies, No. 39 in E^b (K543), No. 40 in G minor (K550) and No. 41 in C major (K551), later known as the "Jupiter". Mozart composed all three symphonies in the space of six weeks. His achievement is all the more remarkable when it is remembered that during this period his financial circumstances compelled him to write embarrassing begging letters to Michael Puchberg and his 6 month old daughter Theresia died from "intestinal cramps".

Whether Mozart heard any or all of these symphonies has not been ascertained; he gave no more public concerts.

17 IX Währingerstrasse 41

Bruckner

In 1868 Bruckner moved into a first floor apartment in this building. He would live here until 1876 and it was here that he composed his symphonies No. 2 to 5 inclusive. His sister "Nani" moved in with him to act as his housekeeper, but she died in 1870.

Bruckner had succeeded Sechter as a teacher at the Vienna Conservatoire. The Viennese soon became aware of Bruckner's numeromania, or the obsessive-compulsive disorder which compelled him to count more or less everything. A lady acquaintance was unable to wear a particular dress in his presence because he felt obliged to count every sequin.

18 IX Boltzmanngasse 6

Schubert

Between 1810 and 1820 Schubert's brother Ferdinand worked as an assistant and then as a teacher at the orphanage here. He also conducted the school orchestra. Ferdinand lived in an apartment with his new wife.

In 1818 the vice-director of the orphanage died and Ferdinand turned to his brother for a funeral mass in his memory. Franz Schubert obliged with his "German Requiem" (D621) which Ferdinand conducted at the orphanage in September 1818. Ferdinand then admitted to his brother that he had passed off the work as his own composition. Franz was not at all put out by his brother's duplicity.

In 1820 Schubert and some friends, including Johann Senn, were arrested by Metternich's secret police on suspicion of seditious activities. Schubert was released but was deeply traumatised by the incident. Ferdinand and his wife invited Franz to recuperate at their home. While here Schubert composed his Six Antiphons for Palm Sunday in about thirty minutes.

Part of the orphanage was demolished in 1910.

19 IX Grünentorgasse 9-11

Schubert

Until 1913 there stood here the house in which Schubert's father and family moved in 1818. Schubert (senior) had been appointed director of the school in this building.

At the end of 1822 Franz Schubert contracted syphilis and in 1823 he was so ill with the secondary stage of the disease that he was admitted to hospital (see XII: 9). When he left hospital he came here to be looked after by his family.

XIII Währing and Lichtental

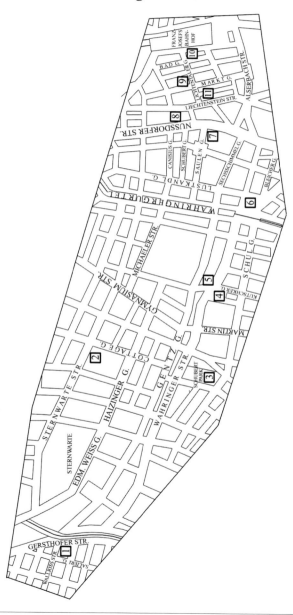

1

XVIII Gersthoferstrasse 55

Bartók

In 1905-6 Béla Bartók lived in this house. The commemorative plaque was provided by the Hungarian government in 1981 to mark the centenary of the composer's birth.

Between New Year and May 1906 Bartók composed here a five-movement orchestral suite in a style which was brash and self-confident. To Bartók's surprise it was a great success at the first performance in Vienna.

XVII Sternwartestrasse 35

Korngold

Erich Korngold was probably the most gifted child prodigy of the twentieth century. In 1906 at the age of nine he played through on the piano his cantata "Gold" to an amazed Mahler, who declared the boy to be a genius. At 11 he composed the ballet *Der Schneemann* which caused a sensation at the Hofoper in 1910.

By 1928 he was a respected composer of piano and chamber music as well as opera. He was also married with a family and in that year he was able to purchase this imposing house in a good area. Shortly after moving in, his wife Luzi gave birth to their second child, which prompted Korngold to compose his charming "Baby Serenade".

In 1934, concerned about the rising tide of anti-semitism in Vienna, the Korngolds moved to Hollywood. Here Korngold turned his talents to film scores, winning Oscars for "The Adventures of Robin Hood" and "Anthony Adverse".

In 1949 the Korngolds returned to Vienna to find the city in ruins and their house occupied by someone else. After a court case their ownership was restored. Here he composed his last opera *Die Kathrin* but it was not a success; Korngold's music was no longer in fashion.

Schubert Park – formerly the Währing Cemetery

In March 1827 a vast throng followed the cortège of **Beethoven** to the Währing Cemetery. At the gates an actor read the funeral oration, written by Franz Grillparzer. Only priests were allowed to speak at the graveside and therefore Beethoven was laid to rest, appropriately, to the sound of silence. For many nights a guard was mounted at the grave to prevent Beethoven's remains suffering the same fate as those of Haydn (see X: 14).

In November 1828 **Schubert** was buried three graves away. Funds were raised for a tombstone which was erected in 1830. The inscription by Grillparzer aroused fierce controversy; "Here music buried a rich possession but even finer hopes". The implication that Schubert did not fully realise his potential upset many Schubertians. *A glance at the list of chamber works that Schubert composed in his last year before his death at 31 suggests that Grillparzer was correct in his judgement.*

During his visit to Vienna in 1838-9 **Schumann** visited the graves. On Beethoven's grave Schumann found an old rusty steel pen. Schumann's fertile imagination decided that the pen had been dropped by Schubert. The pen became one of Schumann's most prized possessions; he used it to compose his Symphony No. 1 (The Spring).

In 1863 the two composers were exhumed and were reburied in metal coffins. Before re-interment the skulls were photographed and all the bones meticulously measured. The cemetery was closed in 1873 and in 1888 it was decided to move the remains of Beethoven and Schubert to the Central Cemetery (Zentralfriedhof, see XVII: B).

To the second exhumation a number of dignataries were invited including, to represent the musical establishment, **Anton Bruckner.** It was an unwise choice; Bruckner's psychological disorders included an unhealthy obsession with human remains. He lost his eye-glass in Beethoven's coffin in his eagerness to view the skeleton, and he clung on to the skull of Schubert until strongly prevailed upon to release it.

In 1923 the cemetery was converted into the Schubert Park. The original gravestones of Beethoven and Schubert remain against the east wall, mercifully free from vandalism or graffiti.

4   St. Lorenz and St. Gertrud Church

Schubert

After the funeral of Schubert at St Joseph's Church in November 1828 (see X: 9) the cortège stopped at the Church of St. Lorenz and St. Gertrud for a second blessing of the composer. The choir of the local Währing school sang the *Miserere* and the *Libera me* before the funeral party moved on to the Währing Cemetery.

5   XVIII Kutschkergasse 44

Schubert

In 1825 Schubert's friend Franz von Schober, in slightly reduced circumstances, entered one of his occasional episodes of paid employment with a printing company. He and his mother took rooms at the inn "Zum Biersack".

Schubert joined his friend here in July 1825 and composed his three Shakespeare settings, including "Hark, Hark the Lark".

The oft-related tale that Schubert composed this song on the back of a menu after being touched by the muse while carousing with friends in the beer garden here is a fiction.

6   Volksoper

The Volksoper opened in 1898 as a theatre for plays but from 1904 it became the "People's Opera". **Zemlinsky** was an early director here. His brother-in-law **Schoenberg's** opera *Die glückliche Hand* received its first performance in 1924 in the Volksoper.

Webern worked here in 1909 as a répétiteur, apparently in an unpaid capacity.

After the Second World War, together with the Theater an der Wien, this theatre provided a temporary home for the Vienna State Opera until the Staatsoper was re-opened in 1955.

The theatre now specialises in operetta, in particular in works by **Strauss (son), Lehár, Millöcker, Rilke** and **Kálmán**. There is seating for 1600.

Tourists visiting the Volksoper for the first time are often puzzled by a periodic rumbling noise which is ignored by regular attendees; the noise is from passing trains on the U6 U-Bahn line on the viaduct behind the theatre.

7   IX Säulengasse 3

Schubert

In 1801 Schubert's father negotiated a mortgage and was able to purchase this small house. The living accommodation was on the first floor and the schoolrooms on the ground floor. When the family moved to this house "Zum schwarzen Rössl" (The Black Horse), Schubert was four years old. In 1803 Schubert became a pupil in his fathers school. His early musical education was in the hands of his father and elder brothers, Ignaz and Ferdinand. In due course a family string quartet was established in which Schubert played the viola. Many of Schubert's early compositions were for this family group.

Between 1808 and 1813 Schubert attended the Stadtkonvict (see III: 9) during which time he returned home only for a brief period each autumn. After training for a year at the college of St. Anna (see II: 23) Schubert returned here both to live and to teach as a school assistant. Not the most motivated of teachers, Schubert was apparently rather quick to raise his hand to recalcitrant pupils.

The plaque over the entrance to the building, which is today occupied by a motor vehicle company, notes that it was here that Schubert composed his setting of Goethe's *Erlkönig*. Although true it gives no indication of Schubert's remarkable musical output when he lived here; of Schubert's 1000 works, over 400 were composed in this house; in 1815 alone there were two symphonies, four operas, two masses, chamber music and many songs.

In 1816 Schubert gave up the profession of teaching and left the parental home to stay with his friend Franz von Schober. Two years later his father moved to Grünentorgasse (see XII: 19)

8   IX Nüssdorferstrasse 54

Schubert

On January 31st 1797 Franz Schubert was born in this house "Zum roten Krebsen" (The Red Crayfish). The birth probably took place in the kitchen alcove, the warmest room in the house. His mother was 40; Franz would be one of only five children of fourteen who would survive infancy.

His father was a respected but far from prosperous schoolmaster. His school was on the ground floor with about 180 day pupils. He was obliged by contract to teach poor children free of charge making what profit he could from the more affluent families.

The Schuberts moved to the Säulengasse in 1801. The upper floor of "Zum roten Krebsen" became a Schubert museum in 1912.

9   Lichtentaler Pfarrkirche

On February 1st 1797 **Franz Schubert** was baptised in this church, which would have an important part to play in his early life.

Schubert came under the tutelage of Michael Holzer, the choirmaster. Holzer taught Schubert the piano, organ and violin and also gave instruction in harmony, counterpoint and thorough-bass. Years later Holzer recalled that, whenever he tried to teach Schubert something new, his pupil knew it already; Holzer could only stare at Schubert in silent wonder.

To celebrate the centenary of the church in 1814 the 17-year-old Schubert composed his Mass No. 1 in F major. Schubert himself conducted the performance. Among those present at this first public performance of a work by Schubert was his teacher **Antonio Salieri.** Schubert also composed his Mass No. 2 in G and his Mass No.3 in C (dedicated to Holzer) for this church.

The organ on which Schubert played is still extant although the console was subsequently replaced. The original console has been preserved and is exhibited in an alcove in the organ loft.

In 1825 the 21-year-old **Johann Strauss (father)** married Anna Streim in this church. Anna's father, who managed a tavern in which Strauss and Lanner performed, was not happy about the matter; music was a notoriously insecure profession. But he had to bow to the inevitable; Anna was already pregnant.

10 IX Badgasse 8

Schubert

Here stood the house and silk-weaving mill of the Grob family. Frau Grob was a widow with two musical children, Heinrich and Therese. She held regular musical evenings here to which both Schubert and Antonio Salieri were frequently invited.

Therese Grob had a beautiful soprano voice and was a soloist in the first performance of Schubert's Mass in F major (see entry above).

She was also Schubert's first serious girl-friend. But Schubert was never able to furnish proof required by the law that he had sufficient means to marry. In 1820 Therese married a master baker in the Lichtental church.

11 IX Liechtensteinstrasse 68 - 70

Schoenberg

Arnold Schoenberg moved to an apartment in this house in 1903 with his wife Mathilde and baby daughter Gertrud. A son Georg was born here in 1904. Mathilde's brother Zemlinsky also lived in this house. After a period when he taught at the Schwarzwaldschule (see V: 19), Schoenberg began to take private pupils at home. Anton von Webern, Alban Berg and Egon Wellesz all made their way here for tuition.

In his music Schoenberg was exploring the world of atonality. His first and second string quartets and his first Chamber Symphony were composed here. At the first of his so-called "Scandal Concerts" (see V: 26) the Viennese expressed their disapproval when these three works were performed at the Bösendorfer Hall in 1907.

But it was his private life which would cause Schoenberg such despair at this time. Another apartment in this house was occupied by the artist Richard Gerstl. Both Schoenberg and his wife developed an interest in art and received lessons from Gerstl; Mathilde also acted as a model.

As tensions in her marriage grew, Mathilde embarked upon an affair with Gerstl which culminated in the pair running away to live together. Friends, led by Webern, approached Mathilde and persuaded her that her duty was to her husband and children. Mathilde returned to Schoenberg. The affair had a tragic sequel: Gerstl committed suicide.

XIV Döbling

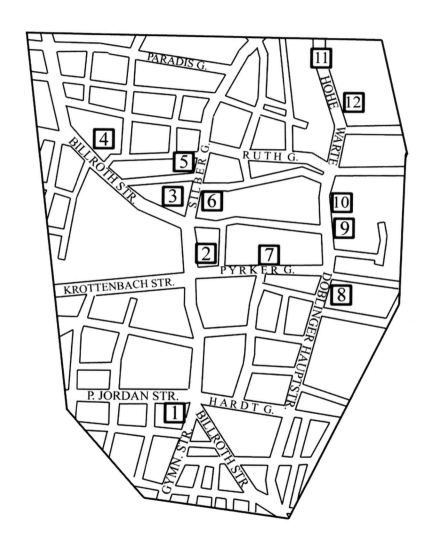

XVIII Gymnasiumstrasse 87

Lanner

On this site stood the house known as "The Cock" where Josef Lanner died in April 1843. He succumbed to a typhus infection at the age of 42, and all Vienna mourned. His friend and rival Johann Strauss (father) conducted at the funeral.

2 XIX Billrothstrasse 68

Wolf

Between 1885 and 1894 Hugo Wolf lived here intermittently as a guest of the Köchert family. It was probably in 1888 that Wolf and Melanie Köchert became lovers. Discretion was of paramount importance; her husband Heinrich, the Imperial Jeweller, was a man of wealth and influence.

Perhaps it was the affair with Melanie that prompted Wolf to begin composition of the *Italienisches Liederbuch* here, although after composing six songs of Volume I his muse deserted him for a whole year. He was suffering from the symptoms of secondary syphilis which he had contracted from a prostitute a few years earlier. At the end of 1891 he recovered and completed the remaining fifteen songs of Volume I in less than a month.

3 Rudolphinerhaus Clinic

Mahler

Brahms's friend Theodor Billroth was associated with this hospital which still maintains a good reputation.

In June 1898 Gustav Mahler, in his early days as director of the Hofoper, underwent major surgery for the removal of haemorrhoids. Three years later Mahler suffered a recurrence and nearly died from the ensuing haemorrhage.

4 Strauss-Lanner Park

In April 1803, 20,000 Viennese followed the coffin of **Josef Lanner** to the former Döbling Cemetery. Here his erstwhile friend and rival **Johann Strauss (father)** conducted the 1st Citizens' Regiment Band at the graveside.

In September 1849 Strauss himself had an even more magnificent funeral. Over 100,000 lined the streets from St. Stephen's Cathedral, where the funeral service had been held, to the Döbling Cemetery. His coffin was carried by members of his orchestra. Behind the coffin the leader of the orchestra carried a black cushion on which lay Strauss's violin with its strings cut. At the graveside Strauss's last waltz *Wanderers Lebewohl* ("Wanderer's Farewell") was played. It was an emotional occasion.

In 1904 the remains of Lanner and Strauss were exhumed and reburied in the Central Cemetery. The original gravestones were preserved and remain today. In 1927 the cemetery was closed and became the Strauss-Lanner Park.

5   XIX Silbergasse 9

Beethoven

Beethoven spent the summer of 1821 in rooms in the building preceding the present one. He was recuperating from a severe attack of jaundice and struggling to complete his *Missa Solemnis*.

6   XIX Silbergasse 4

Beethoven

Beethoven stayed in the house that occupied this corner site during the late summer and autumn of 1815. Here he completed his two Sonatas for Cello and Piano (Opus 102).

Schubert

In the garden of this house there took place in August 1827 the first performance of Schubert's beautiful part-song *Ständchen* (Serenade) D920, a setting of words by Franz Grillparzer.

The song had been requested by his friend Anna Fröhlich, the director of the Gesellschaft der Musikfreunde's singing school, as a surprise birthday gift for a student of the school, Louise Gosmar.

This young lady, the fiancée of Schubert's friend and patron Leopold Sonnleithner, was staying at this house with friends.

Anna Fröhlich planned the surprise performance carefully. As darkness fell she and her pupils drove in three carriages to Döbling. A piano was quietly positioned beneath Louise's window. Josephine Fröhlich, who was to sing the alto solo, and the girls choir silently moved into position. The plan went awry when Schubert failed to arrive; he had forgotten that he was supposed to be there. Another pianist was drafted in and Schubert missed the first performance of one of his loveliest songs.

7 XIX Pyrkergasse 13

Beethoven

Beethoven spent the summer of 1822 here while completing his *Missa Solemnis*. It was here that Beethoven revealed a remarkable capacity for duplicity in his dealings with music publishers.

He had promised the Mass to the publishing house of Simrock. In May 1822 Simrock gently mentioned to Beethoven that more than a year had elapsed since the composer had promised to send him a copy of the score. Beethoven, aware of the stature of his Mass, then informed Simrock that he was negotiating with four other publishers. When Simrock politely reminded Beethoven that he had already paid a deposit to the composer, Beethoven fobbed him off with a promise to compose another Mass, a pledge which he failed to honour.

8 XIX Döblinger Haupstrasse 76-8

Casino Zögernitz

Here stood the Biedermeier-style casino and garden which was immensely popular with the Viennese in the middle of the nineteenth century. Many concerts were given here and **Johann Strauss (son)** was a regular performer.

9　XIX Döblinger Haupstrasse 92

Beethoven

Beethoven lived in this former vine grower's cottage in the summer of 1803. If the recollection of his pupil Ferdinand Ries is correct he also lived here in the summer of 1804.

Here Beethoven worked on his "Eroica Symphony", which was dedicated to his hero Napoleon Bonaparte. When Bonaparte declared himself Emperor of France in 1804 Beethoven withdrew the dedication by defacing the title page.

In all probability Beethoven also composed his Piano Sonata Op 53 (the "Waldstein") here.

Although the building has been modified considerably since Beethoven's time, the four rooms that he occupied have been restored as a museum. The name of the house, "Biederhof", refers to a later owner.

10　XIX Döblinger Haupstrasse 96

Villa Wertheimstein

In 1870 the Jewish financier Leopold von Wertheimstein purchased this villa from a wealthy Viennese industrialist. Here Josephine von Wertheimstein and her daughter Franziska played hostesses to the rich and famous in one of the most celebrated salons in Vienna.

Guests included the painter Hans Makart and the dramatist Eduard von Bauernfeld, Schubert's friend, who died in a cottage in the park in 1890. Recitals were given by Ferruccio Busoni and the Russian pianist and composer Anton Rubinstein.

The villa, with its staircase frescos by Schubert's friend Moritz von Schwind, was left to the city by Franziska and is now the Museum of Döbling.

11   Hohe Warte

Mahler

In November 1901 Gustav Mahler became engaged to Alma Schindler in the Hohe Warte. The couple had walked from Alma's family home in Heiligenstadt (see XV: 6) to the Döbling post office in order that Mahler could make a telephone call. On their way back, walking up the snow-covered hill in total silence, Mahler suddenly made his unconventional "proposal" which Alma related in her memoirs: "It is not easy to marry a man like me! I must be entirely free. I cannot allow myself to be hindered by mundane responsibilities".

Alma, taken aback by Mahler's implicit assumption of her acceptance and his statement of terms, could only lamely remind Mahler that she came from a family of artists. (Her step-father was the artist Karl Moll).

Alma would soon have further experience of her fiancé's dictatorial attitude; although she was a composition pupil of Zemlinsky, Mahler forbade her to compose.

12   XIX Hohe Warte 32

Webern

Between 1925 and 1931 Anton von Webern taught at the Israelite Institute for the Blind here. This school accepted blind Jewish children from countries as far as Poland and Hungary. Webern's duties included conducting the school choir on a twice-weekly basis, and he also gave piano lessons. He was often deeply moved by his pupils' dedication and determination to overcome their handicap.

XV Grinzing, Heiligenstadt and Nüssdorf

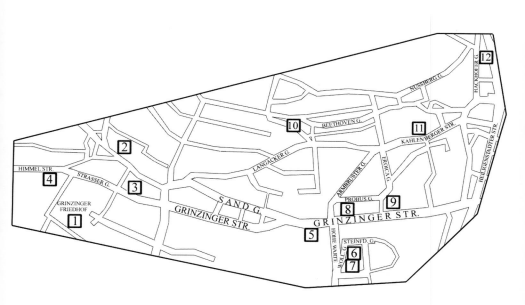

1   Grinzing Cemetery

After his death in May 1911 at the age of 50 **Gustav Mahler** was buried in this cemetery, Group 6, row 7 No. 1; the same grave in which his daughter Maria Anna ("Puzi") had been interred in 1906. She died from diphtheria at the age of 4.

Mahler had requested a simple funeral with no words or music. Many hundreds were present including Schoenberg and his disciples Berg and Webern, and also the conductor Bruno Walter.

The gravestone was designed by his friend Josef Hoffmann. In accordance with Mahler's wishes the headstone was inscribed only with the composer's name; "Those who seek me will know who I was, the rest do not need to know".

His widow Alma is buried elsewhere in the cemetery. She died in 1964 at the age of 85.

Also buried in this cemetery is the pianist **Paul Wittgenstein,** brother of the philosopher Ludwig. Wittgenstein lost his right arm in the First World War. Showing extraordinary resilience and determination to overcome his handicap, he commissioned piano works for the left hand only from the leading composers of the day. Richard Strauss, Prokofiev, Britten and Korngold all composed works for him. The best known (and best) is Ravel's Concerto for the Left Hand.

2   XIX Cobenzlgasse 22

Stolz

A commemorative plaque on the "Heurigen Reinprecht" records that Robert Stolz composed his song *Ich bin in Grinzing einheimisch* here in 1938, just before the annexation of Austria by Germany forced him to flee his homeland.

3   XIX Himmelstrasse 4

Eysler

Edmund Eysler also went into hiding after the *Anschluss* when his works were banned. In this charming little house he composed his operetta *Bruder Straubinger* in 1903. It was a big success in Vienna but has failed to make an impact elsewhere.

| 4 | **XIX Himmelstrasse 25** |

Schubert

A plaque here notes that Schubert was "often and happily" in Grinzing. Schubert loved Grinzing with its wooded walks and streams, and he was very partial to the "Heurige", the tart new wine of the area. Schubert tended to drink far more of this wine than was good for him. It was after a heavy drinking session in Grinzing that Schubert became involved in an unpleasant scene in which he verbally abused two hapless orchestral musicians who were simply enjoying polite conversation with him.

| 5 | **XIX Grinzingerstrasse 64** |

Beethoven

Beethoven spent the summer of 1808 in this house in which he completed his "Pastoral Symphony". It was during his stay here that Beethoven revealed his volatile and eccentric personality.

Beethoven had rented rooms on the street side of the house. In rooms facing the garden lived the young Franz Grillparzer, then 17, and his mother. This lady was a great lover of music and when Beethoven was playing the piano in his room she stood in the corridor between the apartments to listen. One day Beethoven, sensing her presence, opened his door to find her there. He stormed out of the house and refused to play the piano there again.

| 6 | **XIX Steinfeldgasse 8** |

Mahler

In 1901 Alma Schindler, Mahler's future wife moved into this then new house with her mother and step-father, the painter Karl Moll. It was in this house and garden that many meetings of the

Secession Movement took place. The secessionists were led by Gustav Klïnt who also had designs upon Alma.

Mahler took a keen interest in the new artistic movement and commissioned one of its early presidents, Alfred Roller, to design the sets of a new production at the Hofoper of *Tristan und Isolde*. After this acclaimed production Mahler appointed Roller director of design at the Hofoper.

There were also many musical evenings at this house with Mahler present; another frequent guest was the composer Hans Pfitzner.

7   XIX Wollergasse 10

Mahler

In 1906 the architect Josef Hoffman designed this house for Karl Moll. Four years later Hofmann would be asked to design Mahler's gravestone.

Mahler stayed here during his visits to Vienna in his last years. This address also appears on his death certificate.

8   XIX Probusgasse 6

Beethoven

Beethoven stayed in this house in the summer and early autumn of 1802. He composed the three Piano Sonatas (Opus 31) and the three Violin Sonatas (Opus 30) here.

He also completed his Symphony No. 2 in D major. The sunny optimism of this symphony belies Beethoven's mental state at this time. He had for some years been aware that his hearing was becoming progressively impaired. During this summer in Heiligenstadt he realised that his deafness would eventually end his career as a concert pianist. His despair culminated in the so-called "Heiligenstadt Testament" of October 1802.

In this curious document the 31-year-old composer poured out his soul to his two brothers. He revealed that at one point he had contemplated suicide. Although Beethoven never sent the testament, (it was found among his belongings after his death), it does seem to have acted as a catharsis for him. From 1803 onwards he appeared to have come to terms with his affliction.

The house has been restored as a museum.

9   XIX Pfarrplatz 2

Beethoven

Beethoven lived in the "Schlögelsches Haus" in May and June 1817. The house dates from the seventeenth century. Beethoven moved lodgings frequently at this stage in his life, which was dominated by litigation to obtain sole guardianship of his nephew Karl.

10   XIX Beethoven Ruhe

Beethoven habitually strolled along the stream which today is a suburban brook, the Beethovengang. Tradition has it that Beethoven rested against a tree here listening to the birdsong which he incorporated into his "Pastoral Symphony", although by 1808 when he composed the symphony his hearing had deteriorated to such an extent that it is unlikely that he was able to distinguish different birdsongs. The place is marked by a bust by Anton Fernkorn, dating from 1883.

11   XIX Kahlenberger Strasse 26

Beethoven

In this attractive eighteenth century house with its Rococo façade, Beethoven lived in July and August 1817. He was much preoccupied by legal proceedings over the custody of his nephew Karl.

It was here that he received, through his former pupil Ferdinand Ries, an offer to compose two symphonies for the Philharmonic Society of London. It was suggested that he would travel to London the following winter to give concerts on behalf of the Society. Beethoven accepted but then declined on health grounds.

Schikaneder, Lehár

This beautiful eighteenth century mansion was modified in the early nineteenth century. The house was owned by Emmanuel Schikaneder, the librettist of Mozart's "Magic Flute". He lived here from 1802 until 1812, the year in which he died in poverty.

Franz Lehár bought the house in 1932. The following year he composed *Giuditta* here. During the Second World War Lehár and his wife lived at their villa in Bad Ischl. On their return to Vienna in 1944 Lehár discovered that the Schikaneder-Schlössel had been ransacked by looters who had removed his books, scores and personal papers.

The house now has a small private museum. A plaque commemorates the wedding of the tenor Richard Tauber in the house chapel.

XVI Around Schönbrunn

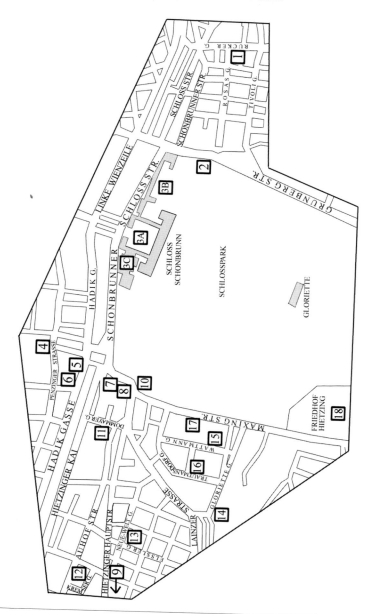

1 XII Ruckergasse 12

Webern

In February 1911 Anton von Webern married Wilhelmine
Mörtl, his first cousin, (their mothers were sisters). They married
in a civil ceremony in Danzig. The closeness of the relationship
prompted deep misgivings on the part of both families, and the
couple were unable to celebrate their union in the Catholic Church
until granted a special papal dispensation. This second ceremony
took place in the parish church of Ober St. Veit in 1915, by which
time they had three children.

The families of the couple were also upset because Wilhelmine
was seven months pregnant when the civil marriage took place.
Nevertheless Wilhelmine's parents allowed the couple and their new
daughter to stay with them in their apartment while the Weberns
were in Vienna.

2 Grünbergstrasse/Schönbrunnerstrasse – Xaipe Villa

Beethoven

One of the more curious traits of the Viennese was their relish
for "contests" between the great virtuosi of the day, exemplified by
Mozart's meeting with Clementi (see V: 1D). In his early days in
Vienna, Beethoven was involved in a number of these spurious
competitions. After competing against Beethoven, the Abbé Gellinek
declared Beethoven to be a devil; "He will play us all to death". After
being crushed by Beethoven at another "contest" Daniel Steibelt
swore that he would never meet Beethoven again.

At his delightful Xaipe Villa Baron Raymond von Wetzlar
offered hospitality to artists of all persuasions during the summer
months. The cultured Wetzlar was a staunch patron of the pianist
Josef Wölffl. In 1799 Wetzlar invited Prince Lichnowsky to bring
his young protégé Beethoven to the villa for a "contest" between the
two virtuosi. Wölffl, a kind and courteous man, was a pianist of the
Mozartean School with neat accurate playing.

Beethoven, exploiting the increased range and power of the new pianoforte to the full, was sensational.

3   Schönbrunn Palace and Park

A   Schönbrunn Palace

The great architect J.B. Fischer von Erlach's original conception was greatly scaled down before construction began in 1696 of this splendid Baroque building. It was the favourite residence of Empress Maria Theresa who lived here in the summer.

The boys of the choir of St. Stephen's often performed at the Palace. In 1740, when **Josef Haydn** joined the choir, the constructors' scaffolding was still in place. The choir boys incurred the displeasure of the Empress by climbing the scaffolding and making a great din as they did so. Although forbidden to play on the scaffolding by order of the Empress, Haydn was unable to resist the temptation and received a thrashing for his pains.

On an afternoon in October 1762 The Empress received the six-year-old **Mozart**, together with his sister Nannerl and his parents. The two children played the harpsichord for the Imperial family, probably in the Mirror Room.

Two incidents have become legendary; at one point Mozart jumped on to the lap of the Empress and "kissed her thoroughly"; and during a tour of the palace accompanied by two of the Archduchesses Mozart slipped over on a polished floor. On being helped to his feet by one of the daughters of the Empress, Mozart thanked her for her kindness and proposed marriage! But the Archduchess was Marie-Antoinette, later Queen of France, and history had a different fate in store for her.

B   The Orangerie

In February 1786 Emperor Josef II gave a dinner in honour of the Governor General of Austrian Netherlands; there were 82 guests. The long Orangerie, only part of which still exists, was the only room in the palace that could be heated efficiently.

For this occasion the Emperor had commissioned two operas. After the banquet the guests moved to one end of the room where **Mozart** directed the première of his one-act singspiel *Der Schauspieldirektor*. At the end the guests repaired to the other end of the room where **Salieri** waited to direct his opera buffo *Prima la musica, e poi le parole*.

C   The Schlosstheater

This is the oldest surviving theatre in Vienna, dating from 1747. Beautifully restored, it is used by the Kammeroper (see IV: 13) in the months of July and August.

Both **Mozart** and **Haydn** gave concerts here. In November 1781 Mozart attended a gala performance here of *Alceste* by **Gluck**.

4   XIII Penzingerstrasse 82

Webern

Anton Webern moved into a first floor apartment in this house with his family in January 1932. Tired of constantly commuting from Mödling to Vienna for his increasing number of conducting commitments, Webern was delighted to find this attractive house with its large garden.

But within two weeks Webern found himself unable to concentrate on his work because of noise from the street beneath his study window. That Webern was so easily distracted by normal street sounds is an indication of his fragile mental health. More than once in that year Webern fainted at the podium and complained of severe stomach pains which, after investigation, were found to be of psychosomatic origin. In the summer of 1932 the family returned to Mödling.

5   XIII Hadikgasse 62

Beethoven

Beethoven took a room in the "Hadik Schlössel" on May 1st 1824, intending to stay here for the whole summer. After three weeks he left abruptly, complaining that people on a wooden footbridge across the River Wien stared at him while he was shaving. The house still stands, but where the footbridge crossed the river is now the Kennedybrücke with its important interchange for buses, trams and the underground.

6   XIII Hadikgasse 72

Wagner

In May 1863 Wagner rented a large apartment on the first floor of this attractive villa from its owner, Baron van Woclow. Here he composed much of *Die Meistersinger von Nürnberg*. Money was no object to Wagner, even though he seldom had any, but when he furnished his new rooms he surpassed himself. The walls were lined in silk, the floors covered in heavy rugs with ankle-deep pile and all seats had expensive covers and cushions.

In February 1864 Johannes Brahms, who was then 30 and just beginning to establish himself in Vienna, was invited to attend a musical evening at Wagner's apartment. Although Brahms's great mature works were still in the future Wagner was fully aware of the younger composer's rising reputation and also that he had the support of the acclaimed but much-feared critic Eduard Hanslick. In *Die Meistersinger* Wagner lampooned Hanslick mercilessly in the character of the pedantic Sixtus Beckmesser, a cruel caricature of the critic.

Wagner greeted Brahms affably and invited him to play. Brahms performed his "Handel Variations". Wagner's remark at the conclusion of Brahms's performance is well documented. "It shows what can be done with the old forms by someone who knows how to use them". Whether Wagner spoke in admiration or with barbed condescension is not clear.

Inevitably Wagner's profligacy caught up with him; In March 1864, as his creditors closed in, Wagner was obliged to perform a "moonlight flit", according to some accounts disguised in female clothing.

---

7 · XIII Hietzinger Haupstrassse 10-14 – Dommayer's Kasino

Johann Strauss (son)

The Parkhotel Schönbrunn today stands on the site of Dommayer's Kasino which was an elegant building in classical style. It included a casino, a dance hall and a concert hall.

Johann Strauss (father) had many successes here, including the first performance of his "Elizabethan Waltz" (Op 71). Three weeks before his death in April 1843 Josef Lanner made his final appearance here.

But it was the début in October 1844 of Johann Strauss (son) with his own orchestra which created the greatest sensation. Aided by his mother, who had been estranged from the elder Strauss for some years, Strauss arranged a "soirée dansante" in the beautifully decorated concert hall. The Viennese were intrigued by Strauss's perceived impertinence in establishing an orchestra in rivalry with his famous father. The hall was packed.

Strauss's programme included newly-composed waltzes *Gunstwerber Walzer* (Op 4) and *Sinngedichte Walzer* (Op 1), which were encored many times. The evening was a triumph.

8 · XII Hietzinger Hauptstrasse 6

Berg

Alban Berg lived in this small house, the house of an aunt, for two years from 1905. He was employed as a civil servant in the capacity of a trainee accountant.

During this period he was a pupil of Arnold Schoenberg. Although he had composed a few songs in his youth he had received no formal musical tuition until he met Schoenberg in 1904 at the age of 19.

9 · XIII Hietzinger Hauptstrasse 113

Schoenberg

Arnold Schoenberg lived in this house with his first wife Mathilde and their children in the years 1910 and 1911. Here he composed much of his opera *Die glückliche Hand,* although it would not be performed until 1924. He also began to write his textbook "The Theory of Harmony".

These were times of severe financial hardship for Schoenberg. Friends, led by Webern, rallied round to raise funs for him and Schoenberg made a direct appeal to Gustav Mahler for financial help to support his family. Mahler responded by sending twice the requested amount. In 1911 his financial predicament and rising anti-Semitism in Vienna prompted him to move to Berlin.

10 Am Platz; Hietzinger Pfarrkirche, Mariä Geburt

Berg

In this church, the favourite of Empress Maria Theresa, Alban Berg and his wife Helene married according to the rites of the Catholic Church in 1915. They had first married at the Protestant church in the Dorotheergasse (see V: 17) in 1911.

11 XIII Dommayergasse 1 – Café Dommayer

A plaque commemorates the meeting in Dommayer's coffee house of the "The Golden Age" and "Silver Age" of operetta. In 1899, the year of his death, **Johann Strauss (son)** met the 19-year-old **Robert Stolz** who was just setting out on his own distinguished career.

12 XIII Kremsergasse 1

Webern

In August 1913 Anton von Webern moved into a small apartment in the building which stood here with his wife and two small children. The apartment comprised two rooms, kitchen and bathroom.

This was a difficult year for Webern; He had just completed a prolonged course of psychiatric treatment and, in March, had endured the infamous "Skandalkonzert" in the Musikverein (see XVI: A) when his "Six Pieces for Orchestra" were received by the audience with unsuppressed mirth.

13   XIII Elsslergasse 26

Schmidt

This was the residence of the Hungarian-born Franz Schmidt, one of the most unjustly neglected of composers. Schmidt's lifespan (1874-1939) encompassed some of the most rapid and far-reaching changes in the structures and forms of music in the history of the art and this is reflected in Schmidt's music. There are echoes of late Brahms, Reger, Richard Strauss and Schoenberg in his music which nonetheless has an individuality very much its own.

Schmidt was one of the few to escape unscathed after a confrontation with Gustav Mahler during the latter's tenure as Director of the Hofoper. Schmidt was a cellist in the Vienna Philharmonic Orchestra which also played at the Hofoper. Mahler preferred Schmidt to play the solo passages although he refused to pay Schmidt more than the salary due to a rank and file player. When Schmidt protested, Mahler lost his temper and ordered Schmidt to play the solo cello parts in that evening's performance of *Die Walküre*.

Sticking to his guns Schmidt pointedly took a seat on the back deck of the cello section. Mahler affected not to notice and did not refer to the episode again.

14   XIII Gloriettegasse 43

Schoenberg

This small house was owned by Silvia "Lili" Lieser, a wealthy friend of Alma Mahler. It was at Alma's instigation that the financially hard-pressed Schoenberg family was offered the use of the house, gratis, an offer of which they availed themselves from 1908 until 1910.

These were traumatic times for the Schoenbergs. Earlier in 1908 Mathilde Schoenberg had left her husband to live with the painter Richard Gerstl (see XIII: 11). She was persuaded to return to Arnold and Gerstl subsequently committed suicide. Mathilde withdrew into herself; visitors to this house remember her sitting hunched in a corner, morose, taciturn and contributing nothing to the household chores.

Schoenberg, deeply traumatised by the betrayal of his wife and former best friend, embarked upon his monodrama *Erwartung*. Although Schoenberg remained silent on any connection between his own personal angst and this searing work, it is difficult to believe that his own devastation is not reflected in the score.

Schoenberg returned to this house in 1915, once again on a rent-free basis, awaiting his call-up orders. He remained until 1917 when be became involved in a dispute with Lili Lieser, who wished to sell the house.

[15]   XIII Wattmanngasse 25

Foerster

The Prague-born composer Josef Bohuslav Foerster lived in this house from 1908 until 1918. He had moved to Vienna from Hamburg with his wife, the operatic soprano Berta Lauterer, who became a great favourite at the Hofoper. Foerster made a living as a music critic.

He was a prolific composer with five operas and five symphonies to his name. Among the works composed here were his suite "From Shakespeare" (Op 76) and his symphonic poem "Springtime and Desire" (Op 93).

In 1918, after the creation of the new state of Czechoslovakia, Foerster returned to Prague as Director of the Conservatoire.

[16]   XIII Trautmansdorfgasse 27

Berg

Alban Berg lived in a first floor apartment in this house from

1911, shortly after his marriage to Helene Nahowski, until his death at the age of 50 in 1935. The apartment comprises an entrance hall, drawing room, kitchen, one bedroom and a bathroom.

Here Berg composed most of his music, from 1923 embracing his teacher Schoenberg's 12-tone method of composition. The unexpected success of his opera *Wozzeck* enabled him to purchase a Ford car.

In 1929 Berg began the composition of his opera *Lulu*. At his death in 1935 he had completed, in full score, the first two acts with the final act still in short score. His widow Helene, bitter at what she perceived as inadequate treatment of her husband in hospital, withheld the score and it was only after her death in 1976 that Friedrich Cerha was allowed to complete the work.

Helene's bitterness would have been the more intense had she been aware of her late husband's long-standing affair with Hanna Fuchs-Robettin, a relationship portrayed by Berg in his "Lyric Suite" for string quartet.

The apartment is today the Alban Berg Stiftung.

17 XIII Maxingstrasse 18

Johann Strauss (son)

Johann Strauss (son) lived with his first wife Henriette (Jetty) in this attractive villa overlooking the Schönbrunn Park from 1870 until 1878. Here Strauss composed his most famous operetta *Die Fledermaus*. Among his other works associated with this house were *Der Carneval in Rom* and *Cagliostro in Wien*.

By 1878 the Strauss' marriage was in difficulties, the underlying reason being the age difference between the couple. Jetty was approaching sixty but looked (and probably felt) older. Strauss, seven years her junior, was at the height of his fame and surrounded by adoring women. Jetty heard rumours and was resigned to the knowledge that Strauss was taking his pleasures elsewhere.

The final crisis was prompted by a startling event. A young man arrived at the villa declaring himself to be Jetty's son. Jetty had been less than frank with Strauss about her past. Strauss knew and accepted Jetty's two daughters from her relationship with a Viennese banker but seemingly was unaware of the existence of Jetty's five other illegitimate children. Strauss's shock was compounded by anger when the young man made a crude attempt to blackmail the composer.

The effect on Jetty was devastating. Soon after, she received a letter from her son (contents unknown), which caused her such distress that she suffered a catastrophic stroke which led to her death on the same evening. That night Strauss left the villa never to return.

18   Hietzing Cemetery

In this cemetery is found the grave of **Alban Berg** (Group 49 No. 24F) who died in 1935 of septicaemia following an infected insect bite. At the graveside Ernst Krenek gave the oration. Egon Wellesz and Stefan Zweig were also present. Helene Berg did not attend.

The painter Gustav Klimt and the dramatist Franz Grillparzer are also buried here. This cemetery is also the final resting place of two ladies who died in sad circumstances. Jetty Strauss was buried here, (her husband was not present) and Melanie Köchert, the long-standing and loyal lover of Hugo Wolf, is interred in a family vault.

XVII St. Marx Cemetery and the Zentralfriedhof

These cemeteries are on the route of tram No 71 from the Schwarzenbergplatz. To visit St. Marx, get off at Landstrasser Hauptstrasse and a brisk ten-minute walk up Leberstrasse will find the cemetery on the right side. For the inappropriately-named Central Cemetery, alight at Zentralfriedhof-Tor 2.

A   The Cemetery of St. Marx

This cemetery was laid out in 1784 and finally closed and deconsecrated in 1874. Notwithstanding the close proximity of an elevated urban motorway the cemetery has an air of quiet melancholy which is emphasised by the brooding old trees, the dense lilac bushes and the ageing Biedermeier monuments.

Mozart was buried here in December 1791, five years after his third child was also interred here; Johann Thomas Leopold Mozart died after just four weeks of life. After the closure of the graveyard around St. Stephen's cathedral St Marx became the parish cemetery.

Mozart's burial

The myths and legends surrounding the death and funeral of Mozart were examined in Chapter I. Conspiracy theories abounded also with regard to the interment. These were refuted by Dr Carl Bär in his sound and well-researched treatise *Mozart: Krankheit, Tod, Begräbnis, (1967).*

According to Bär, Mozart's corpse arrived at the cemetery as darkness began to fall on December 7th 1791. The lateness of the hour almost certainly precluded interment that evening; the burial would have taken place on the following morning. Today the consensus of opinion is that the coffin arrived at the cemetery on December 6th and the burial took place on the 7th.

Contrary to almost universal belief, Mozart did not receive a "pauper's funeral"; his funeral was of the third class, the standard one of the time. Under the reforms of Josef II, funerals were carried out in accordance with the principles of thrift and sound hygienic practice. The deceased was removed from the deathbed as soon as decently possible and buried in a cemetery well away from residential areas, wrapped in a readily biodegradable material such as a linen sack. After interment the process of decomposition was accelerated by the addition of quicklime. The grave would be shared with five or six other corpses. No headstones were allowed, although it was permitted to place a plaque on the wall of the cemetery.

This was the fate of Mozart's body. It did rest in a wooden coffin on its journey from St. Stephen's but was then deposited in the grave wrapped in cloth; the coffin was available for re-use.

It was not until the anniversary of Mozart's death in 1856 that thought was given to a permanent memorial, by which time those with knowledge of the site of Mozart's grave were also dead. In 1868 a bronze sculpture by Hans Gasser was placed in a position which officials believed to be the site of Mozart's grave, but based on pure guesswork. After damage by vandalism this monument was moved to the Zentralfriedhof.

The Curator of the cemetery then took it upon himself to erect a monument utilising fragments from broken gravestones, a memorial which has stood until this day.

Although it is situated only approximately where Mozart was buried it does provide a tangible symbol for the devotees of Mozart who come here.

Two mysteries remain: why did not Baron von Swieten, Mozart's patron who made the funeral arrangements, seek the aid of fellow Freemasons to provide a more fitting memorial to a fellow lodge-member and court composer? And why did his widow Constanza not visit the cemetery for the first time until seventeen years after Mozart's death, and then only at the behest of her second husband?

Two other composers associated with Mozart's last days are also buried in St. Marx.

Johann Albrechtsberger became Kapellmeister at St. Stephen's after Mozart's death. Mozart had been appointed to the post only seven months previously. Albrechtsberger was given a second-class funeral; that is in an individual grave (No. 35) with a headstone.

Franz Süssmayr, Mozart's pupil who completed the Requiem, died from a combination of tuberculosis and alcoholism in 1803 at the age of 37. He was buried in a pauper's grave, a mass burial pit paid for by the parish.

Also interred here is **Anton Diabelli** who began life as a mediocre composer before finding his true *métier* in music publishing. Beethoven and Schubert were among his clients.

His main claim to fame came in 1819. He asked a number of different composers each to compose a variation on a rather mundane waltz-tune that he had written. He planned to publish the variations under the title of *Vaterländischer Künstlerverein* (Society of Artists of the Fatherland). Beethoven refused to be involved in what he described as a "cobbler's patch" of a tune, but then was intellectually stimulated by the challenge. The massive "Diabelli Variations" (Op. 120) duly appeared. Scarcely believing his luck, Diabelli published Beethoven's work as part I with the variations by the other composers including Liszt and Schubert as part II.

Josef Strauss, the second of the three sons of Johann Strauss (father) was buried here in 1870. His remains were subsequently exhumed and transferred to the Zentralfriedhof.

B.   Zentralfriedhof

This cemetery opened in 1874 and has been progressively extended. Over 2,500,000 people are buried here in over a third of a million graves. Shortly after the inauguration of the cemetery it was decided to create Ehrengräben (graves of honour) for the great and the good; composers, writers, artists and politicians buried elsewhere in Vienna.

Thus **Beethoven** and **Schubert** were transferred from Währing Cemetery, **Josef Strauss** from St. Marx, **Johann Strauss (father)** and **Lanner** from Döbling and **Gluck** from Matzleinsdorf. They were reburied in group 32A which has as its centrepiece Hans Gasser's memorial to Mozart which stood in St Marx. In many cases the original gravestones of the empty tombs were left in situ which occasionally has given rise to confusion.

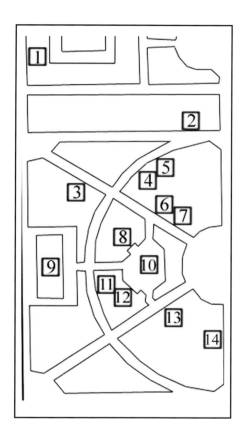

Selection of Composers' graves of honour

1. Schoenberg   2. Ziehrer   3. Eysler

4. Johann Strauss (father)   5. Lanner   6. Johan Strauss (son)

7. Brahms   8. Schubert   9 Gluck

10. Mozart Memorial   11. Wolf   12. Beethoven

13. Suppé   14. Millöcker

In due course **Brahms, Wolf, Johann Strauss (son)** and **Eduard Strauss** were buried here. It is entirely appropriate that Johann Strauss (son) lies buried next to his great friend Brahms. It is also apt, though whether by accident or design is uncertain, that the bust of Wolf which adorns his tomb stares steadfastly in the opposite direction to the bust of Brahms, to whom he showed such antipathy during his lifetime.

Adjacent to this group is group 32C. Here is buried **Arnold Schoenberg**. Schoenberg died in Los Angeles in 1951 and was cremated. In June 1974 his ashes were brought to Vienna and buried in the Zentralfriedhof. His striking gravestone is by the sculptor Fritz Wotruba. Also in this group are buried **Franz Schmidt**, Schoenberg's pupil **Egon Wellesz** and the soprano **Lotte Lehmann**.

Close by are members of the "Silver Age" of operetta; **Ziehrer, Millöcker, Eysler** and **Stolz.** Elsewhere are found the graves of **Antonio Salieri** and **Karl Czerny** (both group O), **Pfitzner** (group 14C) and, in the Evangelical section, **Karl Goldmark**.

Others with musical connections buried here were Brahms's friend Billroth, the critic Eduard Hanslick, the piano maker Ludwig Bösendorf and Ludwig Köchel. Köchel's painstaking compilation of the catalogue of Mozart's works has had remarkably few corrections over the years.

XVIII Baden, Mödling and Perchtoldsdorf

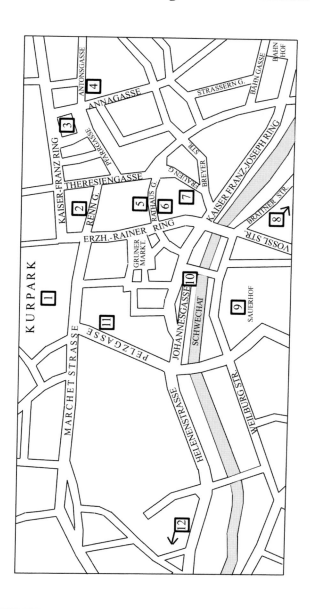

A Baden

Baden lies 18 miles south of Vienna. The curative properties of its sulphurous water, gushing from springs at a temperature of 39° C, have been recognised since Roman times. The patronage of successive Habsburg emperors ensured that Baden became Austria's most important spa town.

Many composers were drawn to this attractive town, in particular it was a favourite of Beethoven.

The operetta composer Millöcker died here in 1899 and the critic Eduard Hanslick's life ended in Baden in 1904.

Perhaps the most enjoyable way of visiting Baden is by the legendary *Lokalbahn* from the Kärntner Ring. This tram follows the Wiedner Hauptstrasse and then wends its way through the southern suburbs of Vienna before arriving in Baden 55 minutes later.

1   Kurpark

These beautiful gardens were laid out in 1792 in honour of the Empress Maria Theresa, who took the waters here. The Strauss-Lanner monument (erected in 1912) commemorates the concerts given here by **Johann Strauss (father)** and **Josef Lanner**. After one such concert in 1830 a newspaper reported that "all Vienna was in Baden; Strauss was Emperor for the night". It was the place to see and be seen for the nobility and wealthy of Vienna.

It is believed that Baden was the "small town of the south of Vienna" that Johann Strauss (son) had in mind as the setting of *Die Fledermaus*.

2   Renngasse 4

Mozart

The plaque affixed to this house stating that Mozart stayed here is misleading: the original house was destroyed during the Great Fire of Baden in 1812 which devastated this area of the town. The house was subsequently rebuilt as a replica of the original. Constanza Mozart "took the cure" in Baden many times, placing a heavy burden upon her husband's financial position. In June 1791 Constanza rented a ground floor apartment of the house, known as "Zum Blumenstock", with her young son Karl. Mozart commuted regularly between Vienna and Baden, where he took another room in the same house. Here on June 18th 1791 he composed *Ave Verum Corpus* (K618).

3   Pfarrkirche St Stephan

Mozart

In this church Mozart directed the first performance of his beautiful motet *Ave Verum Corpus* on July 10th 1791. He had composed the work for Anton Stoll, a schoolteacher who was also choirmaster at this church.

Stoll was a man of great kindness; at the request of Josef Haydn, Stoll took care of Haydn's wife until her death in Baden in March 1800.

4   Antongasse 4

Beethoven

Beethoven lived in this house, "Zum goldenen Schwann", for about six weeks in the early autumn of 1822. Here he composed his overture "The Consecration of the House" for the refurbished Josefstadt Theatre (see XI:14).

5   Rathausgasse 10

Beethoven

This most attractive small eighteenth-century house was Beethoven's most important residence in Baden. Beethoven rented a first floor apartment comprising a bedroom and study from a local coppersmith.

The apartment is now a small museum: among the exhibits is Beethoven's piano by Conrad Graf.

Authorities differ on the number of occasions that Beethoven stayed in this house; he certainly lived here during the summers of 1821 and 1823 and he may also have spent time here in 1822.

Beethoven stayed here for the first time in early autumn 1821 on the advice of his doctor. Beethoven, who was working on the *Missa Solemnis*, had contracted jaundice and his doctor suggested that a visit to the spa would be helpful. Unfortunately the sulphurous waters induced violent diarrhoea and Beethoven returned to Vienna.

In August 1823 Beethoven returned and was joined by his nephew Karl. Here Beethoven completed his string quartets Op130 and Op132 for Prince Galitzin, and also spent considerable time on his ninth symphony.

In October 1823 Beethoven received a courtesy call from Weber, who was in Vienna for the première of *Euryanthe*. On a dismal rainy day Beethoven greeted Weber with a series of bear hugs. Weber noted with astonishment the poverty-stricken room, with everything in hopeless disorder; music, coins and clothing on the floor, the grubby bed unmade, a broken coffee service on the table and the piano with scarcely an unbroken string.

Beethoven's slovenly habits brought him into conflict with his landlord. Beethoven sketched musical ideas on the unvarnished shutters. The landlord demanded that the composer should replace them, although he was not above selling off the old shutters to Beethoven's admirers.

6   Rathausgasse 11

The former inn "Zum schwarzen Adler" ("The Black Eagle")

Two commemorative plaques adorn this building. The first refers to the visit of **Franz Schubert** on 2nd June 1828. Schubert had travelled by coach to Baden with his friend Franz Lachner. During the night at this inn Schubert composed his Organ Fugue in E minor (D952) which he performed at Heiligenkreuz the next day.

The other plaque honours the visits of **Johann Strauss (son)** in 1876 and 1877.

7   Frauengasse 10

Beethoven

Beethoven lived in the "Magdalenahof" briefly in October 1822. He was turning his attention to the "Choral Symphony".

8   Braitner Strasse 26

Beethoven

Beethoven lived in rooms in the "Schloss Braiten" during the summer and autumn of 1816. Earlier in the year Beethoven had been awarded custody of his nephew Karl, although this proved to be just a prelude to a long legal battle with the boy's mother. The composer, sensibly, placed Karl in a private boarding school but decided that this arrangement was unsatisfactory and that the boy should join him in Baden.

In September 1816 the headmaster of the school arrived at the Schloss Braiten with Karl. Although they were expected, Beethoven had made no attempt to bring a semblance of order to his usual domestic chaos. There was no food available and no sleeping arrangements for the guests. Beethoven sported cuts and bruises to his face after an unseemly brawl with a servant. The headmaster could only ponder with misgivings Beethoven's unsuitability as a guardian.

While staying here Beethoven completed his intimate song-cycle *An die ferne Geliebte* and also worked on his Piano Sonata in A (Op101).

9   Weilburgstrasse 11 – "Alter Sauerhof"

Beethoven

In the years 1810 to 1812 Baden was Beethoven's preferred summer retreat and in these years he took rooms in the "Sauerhof".

He arrived in August 1810 in a rueful mood having recently had a proposal of marriage turned down by Therese Malfatti: Beethoven, then 40 had proposed to Therese, aged 19, to the fury of her family.

Therese was the niece of Beethoven's doctor. During this visit Beethoven worked on the String Quartet in F minor (Op95) and began the "Archduke Trio" (Op97).

In 1825 he took Weber for a meal at the Sauerhof.

Salieri

Antonio Salieri was a frequent visitor to Baden between 1786 and 1823, usually staying at the Sauerhof.

☐10 Johannesgasse 10 - 14

Beethoven

Beethoven stayed at the "Johanneshof" in the late Spring of 1807. Here he worked on the Mass in C major.

☐11 Pelzgasse 22

Beethoven

Beethoven stayed in the Schoss Gutenbrunn during the summer and autumn of 1824. It was evidently much to his liking and he was looked after very well.

He worked on the String Quartet in E♭ major (Op. 127) for Prince Galitzin and also negotiated with different publishers for the sale of the *Missa Solemnis*, negotiations which brought his proberty into question.

☐12 The Helenental Valley

The River Schwechat passes through the forested Helenental Valley northwest of Baden. Prominent above the valley are the ruins of the Burg Rauheneck and, opposite, the remains of the Burg Rauhenstein.

The Helenental was a favourite walking place of **Beethoven** (and also of the Imperial family and many more who delight in this pleasant valley).

In July 1826 Beethoven's nephew Karl, in debt and with school examinations looming, walked out to the Rauheneck ruins and attempted suicide. That Karl could discharge two pistols at his own head and escape with superficial injuries suggests that the attempt was half-hearted. Karl soon recovered and was enlisted in the army.

It was inevitable that the consequences of Karl's upbringing from the age of 8, in a dysfunctional family with a possessive and overbearing guardian, would be behavioural problems which went beyond mere youthful rebellion. But Karl's choice of Beethoven's favourite spot for his suicide attempt also suggests that he was not without malice.

B   Perchtoldsdorf

This small town lies a few miles south-west of Vienna in wine-growing country. It was a summer retreat for **Gluck** in his last years. In 1787 and 1791 **Mozart** brought his young son Karl here while he and Constanza went to Prague. Karl was boarded at a private school here.

For many years from 1802 the choirmaster at the fourteenth century church was Ambros Rieder, a prolific composer of church music and a friend of **Schubert**. As a young man, Reider had the privilege of hearing Mozart improvise. His account is worthy of mention: "The bold flight of his fantasy, which soared to the highest regions and then plunged into the depths of the abyss, was something which even the most experienced master of music could not sufficiently admire and wonder at ...... and I move towards my grave in the full conviction that there has only ever been one Mozart".

Brunnergasse 26

Wolf

This was the summer holiday retreat of the Werner family, which became devoted to Hugo Wolf. The Werners offered Wolf the use of the house in order that he would have the solitude to compose.

He came here first in 1888 and set a number poems by Eduard Mörike. The following year he began work on his Spanische Liederbuch. In 1895 he worked on his opera *Der Corregidor* here and also completed the second part of the *Italienische Liederbuch*.

In 1973 the house became the Hugo Wolf museum. The five rooms have been arranged and furnished as they were when Wolf lived here.

Wienergasse 17

Schmidt

Franz Schmidt died at Lohnsteinstrasse 4 in 1939. He had been in poor health for some years, although he managed to complete his Symphony No. 4 in C major in 1935 and his great oratorio "The Book with Seven Seals" in 1937.

At the music school which bears his name in the Knappenhof memorial rooms have been created. Exhibits include his Bösendorfer piano, writing desk and personal items.

C Mödling

Hauptstrasse 79

Beethoven

Mödling was Beethoven's summer retreat in the years 1818 – 1820. In May 1818 he took rooms in this house with his nephew Karl, who was now 12. The legal battle for custody of the boy between his mother and uncle was, not surprisingly, having an effect upon his behaviour. Beethoven entrusted the education of Karl to the parish priest of Mödling, Father Fröhlich. When the priest deemed it necessary to expel the emotionally-disturbed boy for anti-social behaviour, Beethoven was incensed, and he denounced Fröhlich as a drunkard and a libertine. During the summer he completed the mighty Hammerklavier Sonata.

Beethoven returned to the house the following summer of 1819 and worked on the *Missa Solemnis*. His factotum, Anton Schindler, gave a graphic account of Beethoven's usual domestic disorder. Schindler arrived outside the house and heard Beethoven "singing, howling and stamping" parts of the Mass. There had been a quarrel after midnight with the servants which had disturbed the neighbours. The servants had left and Beethoven had gone hungry.

Ashenaugasse 6

Beethoven

Beethoven stayed in this house in the summer of 1820. His landlord in the Hauptstrasse house had refused to allow him to return because of the noise.

The composer was in a relaxed and happy mood. He had finally won custody of his nephew after Karl's mother's final appeal had failed. His contentment is reflected in his Piano Sonata in E major (Op109) which he composed here.

Bernhardtgasse 6

Schoenberg

In 1918 the First World War ended with Vienna in dire straits; food and other essentials were in short supply. Schoenberg moved to an apartment on the first floor of this house. There was a bathroom, hall, sitting-room and glassed in veranda. Today the apartment is the Arnold Schoenberg Memorial Rooms.

Berg and Webern were frequent visitors.

Wienerstrasse 4

Schoenberg

Between 1896 and 1898 Schoenberg conducted a choir, the "Freisinn Choral Society" at the Hotel Bieglerhütte here.

Scheffengasse 8 – Evangelical Church

Schoenberg

In 1924 Schoenberg married his second wife Gertrude, the sister of the violinist Rudolf Kolisch. Schoenberg was 50.

Neusiedlerstrasse 53

Webern

Anton von Webern lived here from 1918 until 1932, to be near his teacher and mentor Arnold Schoenberg. Webern arrived here with his wife and three young children and no money. Menial posts as a *répétiteur* and assistant conductor provided a hand-to-mouth existence for a while. Webern loved the mountains around Mödling; alpine walking was a source of great pleasure to him.

St. Othmar Church

Webern

Webern was conductor of the Mödlinger Männergesangverein. In this church he conducted Schubert's Mass in E^b major (1923) and Bruckner's Mass in F minor (1925).

Im Auholz 8 – Maria Enzersdorf am Gebirge

Webern

In this small village one mile north of Mödling Webern lived from 1932 until his death (at Mittersill) in 1945. The apartment comprised the second floor and the attic.

The house was taken over by the Russian army in 1945 and ransacked.

XIX Salmannsdorf, Dornbach, Hetzendorf and Floridsdorf

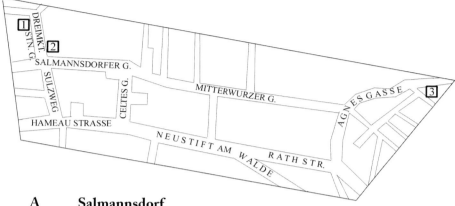

A   Salmannsdorf

1   XIX Dreimarksteingasse 13

Johann Strauss (son)

The Strauss family spent their summer holidays at this house between 1829 and 1836. It was the home of the young Strauss's maternal grandmother. The six-year-old Strauss practised on a small table piano. Here he composed his first waltz which his mother called *Erster Gedanke* (First Thoughts).

2   XIX Dreimarksteingasse 6

Schubert

The commemorative plaque on this house which claims that Schubert stayed here in 1821, and performed his *Das Dörfchen*, is misleading; the present building is of a later date. Schubert's setting of *Das Dörfchen* (The Little Village) became very popular after its first public performance in this year at a charity concert given by the splendidly named "Society of women of nobility to promote the good and the efficacious".

XIX Agnesgasse 9

Flotow

Friedrich von Flotow lived for many years in this house. His best-known opera *Martha* received its first performance at the Kärntnertor Theatre in Vienna in 1847.

B   Dornbach

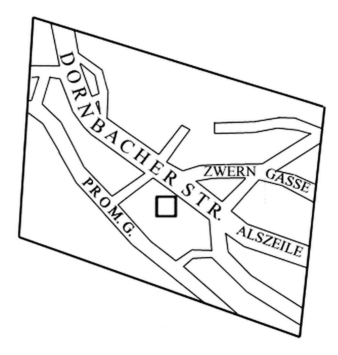

XVII   Dornbacher Strasse 101

Schubert

In late May, June and early July 1827 Schubert stayed at this house, the former inn "The Empress of Austria". He was accompanied by his friend Franz von Schober as he enjoyed a summer sojourn in this wine-growing village on the edge of the Vienna Woods.

Here he began to make sketches for a new opera *Der Graf von Gleichen* (D918), but the opera never came to fruition. He also composed his beautiful song *Das Lied in Grünen* (D917) here.

C   Hetzendorf

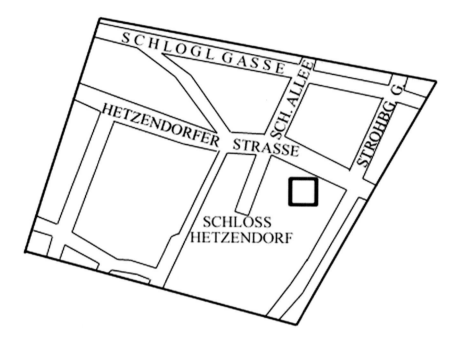

XII   Hetzendorfer Strasse 75A

Beethoven

A small plaque marks the site of the Villa Pronay where Beethoven lived from May until August 1823. Baron Müller had invited Beethoven to live in rooms in his beautiful villa for the summer. Müller was a gentleman attendant at the Imperial Court and it was perhaps his position which accounted for his obsequious habit of bowing to Beethoven whenever he met the composer, a mannerism which annoyed Beethoven intensely.

Beethoven's work on the "Choral Symphony" was interrupted by the arrival of Franz Grillparzer with a new libretto for an opera. Beethoven accepted the libretto of *Melusine* but the project came to nothing.

D.   Floridsdorf

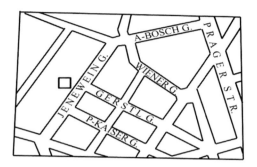

XXI   Jeneweingasse 17

Beethoven

This villa was the home of Countess Anna Marie Erdödy and her husband. The Countess was a fine pianist and a great admirer of Beethoven. The music tutor to the Erdödy family was Josef Linke, a distinguished cellist and it was this which prompted Beethoven to compose his two Cello Sonatas (Op 102) in 1815, which were first performed in this house. These sonatas and the Piano Trios (Op 70) were dedicated to the Countess, an indication of Beethoven's respect for her musicality. Beethoven was a frequent guest here, spending July and August 1815 as a guest of the Erdödys.

The last years of the Countess Erdödy were clouded by scandal; she was the victim of a rumour that she had conspired to murder her son. No charges were ever brought.

XX The Theater an der Wien and the Vienna State Opera

A   Theater an der Wien

This theatre is the oldest in Vienna still extant, with the exception of the Schlosstheater at Schönbrunn. When it opened in 1801 it was a revelation to the Viennese. Its spacious interior had a capacity of over 2000, 700 seated and 1500 standing. The tasteful décor was in a cool blue embellished with silver and the stage boasted state-of-the-art machinery. In comparison the two court theatres, the Burgtheater and the Kärntnertor Theatre, appeared cramped and shabby.

The Theater an der Wien replaced the decrepit Theater auf der Wieden in the old Freihaus (see IX: 6), where Mozart's "Magic Flute" had been premièred ten years before. It was the director of the Freihaus theatre, Emmanuel Schikaneder, who inveigled the authorities into granting him a licence to build its replacement. Schikaneder had been both the librettist and the first Papageno in Mozart's opera. In recognition of this a group of figures depicting Schikaneder as "Pagageno with children" surmounts the so-called "Papageno Gate" on the east side of the Theater an der Wien.

In 1803 Schikaneder invited **Beethoven** to compose an opera on the director's own text, a commission which carried the bonus of free lodgings in the theatre. Beethoven, as the "in-house" composer seized the opportunity to stage a concert of his own works. Beethoven's concept of programming was startling, placing heavy demands on the players, the singers and, not least, the audience.

On that evening in April 1803 the programme included the Symphony No. 1 in C, the first performance of the Symphony No. 2 in D, the Piano Concerto No. 3 in C minor and a new work which Beethoven had written hastily specially for this concert. It was an oratorio "Christ on the Mount of Olives".

Only one rehearsal was possible for this taxing music – on the morning of the concert. It began at 8 o'clock in the morning and by early afternoon everyone was exhausted. Beethoven's patron Prince Lichnowsky came to the rescue, supplying hampers of food and wine and gently persuading the performers to carry on.

The concert received mixed reviews. The orchestral music found favour but the oratorio, which even Beethoven admitted was not his best work, was the subject of criticism.

In 1804 Schikaneder sold his interest in the theatre, releasing Beethoven from his obligation to write an opera for which he had little enthusiasm. He then accepted a libretto by Josef Sonnleithner based on Bouilly's play *Léonore ou l'amour conjugal* which became *Fidelio*. Although he lived in other apartments, Beethoven retained the tenancy of his rooms in the Theater an der Wien, and composed the *Kreutzer* violin sonata and parts of the *Eroica* Symphony here, as well as working on *Fidelio*.

The first performance of Beethoven's only opera took place here in November 1805 exactly one week after the French Army had marched into Vienna to occupy the city. The Imperial family and most of Beethoven's patrons and friends had fled the city. In these inauspicious circumstances *Fidelio* received its first performance. The audience was comprised mostly of uncomprehending French officers. It was a failure and received only two more performances before being withdrawn. It would be eight more years before *Fidelio* was revived, completely revised, and this time it was a success.

In 1808 Beethoven gave another marathon concert at the Theater an der Wien. The programme was once again enormous; first performances were given of the Symphony No. 5 in C minor, the Symphony No. 6 in F (The Pastoral), the Piano Concerto No. 4 in G, parts of the Mass in C and the Scena and Aria *Ah! Perfido*. And as if this was insufficient, Beethoven composed the "Choral Fantasia" (Op 80) for the concert.

The concert was not a success. It was December and the unheated theatre was bitterly cold. The orchestra, which had had hardly any rehearsal, made mistakes and Beethoven loudly abused them in full hearing of the audience. When the "Choral Fantasia" broke down, the furious Beethoven stopped the orchestra and started again. It was not a happy occasion.

When **Rossini** visited Vienna in 1822 he took the city by storm. Performances of his operas were given at the Theater an der Wien which marked the première in the city of "The Barber of Seville", *La Cenerentola* and "The Italian Girl in Algiers". Crowds gathered outside Rossini's hotel and he was obliged to acknowledge the ovation from his balcony.

A composer who sought, in vain, to emulate Rossini's operatic success was **Franz Schubert**. *Die Zauberharfe* was one of fifteen operas that Schubert left in various stages of completion. Few reached the stage and most have been consigned to oblivion. Die Zauberharfe was given eight performances at the Theater an der Wien in the summer of 1820. After the première one observer, Karl Rosenbaum, described the work as "wretched trash".

In 1823 Schubert was invited by Helmina von Chézy to compose incidental music to her new play "Rosamunde, Princess of Cypress." By all accounts the play was an incomprehensible nonsense and was given only two performances before disappearing forever. The script of the play has long since been lost and is remembered only for Schubert's music which was the one aspect of the performance to receive praise.

During his highly successful visit to Vienna in 1845-6 **Hector Berlioz** gave three concerts at the Theater an der Wien. The Frenchman was reverently aware that the podium on which he conducted had been occupied by Beethoven forty years before. Berlioz conducted the "Symphonie Fantasique", the overture "Roman Carnival" and also composed for the concerts two new orchestral songs, *Zaïde* and *Le chasseur danois*.

The attitude of **Richard Wagner** to Vienna was always one of suspicion, a consequence of his varying fortunes there. This was exemplified in 1862 when Wagner gave three concerts at the Theater an der Wien. He conducted orchestral excerpts from *Das Rheingold, Die Walküre* and *Die Meistersinger.* On the one hand Wagner was pleased to acknowledge prolonged applause after each piece but on the other the critics, led by Eduard Hanslick, were universally hostile and the balance sheet showed a considerable financial net loss.

Between 1825 and 1845 opera disappeared from the stage of the Theater an der Wien as the management decided to concentrate on plays, in particular by Johann Nestroy who became the house playwright. When Franz Pokorny became director in 1845 he brought to the post the determination to restore opera in the grand style to this theatre. He started well; he appointed **Franz von Suppé** to the post of conductor and also installed him in an apartment in the theatre building. Suppé composed much music for the stage of the Theater an der Wien, including *Das Pensionat* which is considered to be the first Viennese operetta. But it would not be until 1862 when he moved to the Carltheater (see VI: 23) that Suppé's best work would emerge.

The zenith of Pokorny's tenure was the 1846-7 season when he engaged the soprano Jenny Lind, known as the "Swedish Nightingale". Triumphant though she was in *Norma*, *La Sonnambula* and *Der Freischütz* among others, Lind's financial demands emptied the theatre coffers at an alarming rate.

One of the greatest successes of Pokorny's stewardship was *Zar und Zimmerman* by **Albert Lortzing**. This triumph prompted Pokorny to appoint Lortzing as kapellmeister, joining Suppé in 1845. It was a disaster; the Viennese had no interest in Lortzing's music and he resigned two years later, and was subsequently overtaken by penury and an early death.

Opera as staged in the opulent style of Pokorny's vision is a very expensive undertaking and the severe financial difficulties which soon presented themselves may have contributed to Pokorny's sudden death in 1850. His son Alois who took over as director attempted to run the theatre on more prudent lines but gave up the unequal struggle in 1862.

His successor Friedrich Strampfer, in thrall to the theatre's creditors, turned to the slightly less expensive operatic form, operetta. In 1864 he pulled off a musical coup when he signed a three-year contract with **Jacques Offenbach**. Offenbach's first contribution to the theatre, *Rheinnixon*, was a failure, but that was soon forgotten after *La Belle Hélène* received its first Viennese performance shortly after its première in Paris. Offenbach's time in Vienna would be a precursor to the golden and silver ages of operetta which would dominate the stage of the Theater an der Wien for the next seven decades.

In 1870 **Johann Strauss (son)** signed an exclusive two-year contract with the Theater an der Wien. His first offering was "Inigo and the Forty Thieves" which although popular at the time, has disappeared from the repertoire. A number of Strauss's operettas received their first performances in this house. An exception was "A Night in Venice" after Strauss learnt of his second wife Lili's affair with the theatre director Franz Steiner. Strauss staged the work in Berlin instead where it was a failure. His greatest work *Die Fledermaus* received its première here in 1874. Although not an overwhelming success at its first performance, it is recognised as Strauss's masterpiece.

In 1884, to mark the fortieth anniversary of Strauss's début in Vienna, a grand gala concert was given here in which Strauss conducted excerpts from all his operettas. After being presented with a commemorative medal he made a brief but emotional speech.

Karl Millöcker, in whose honour the street on the east side of the theatre is named, was conductor here for ten years from 1869 and had a triumph in 1882 with *Der Bettelstudent.* **Karl Zeller** made his name here with his operetta *Der Vogelhändler.* Both these works are staged frequently in Vienna at the Volksoper (see XIII: 6).

The "Silver Age" of operetta was launched at the Theater an der Wien in 1905 when **Franz Lehár's** "The Merry Widow" received its première. It was followed in 1909 by "The Count of Luxembourg".

Other directors of this theatre have included **Alexander von Zemlinsky** (1903) and **Robert Stolz** (1907-10).

There was an exception to the dominance of operetta in 1897 when **Puccini** arrived at the theatre to supervise the first Viennese performance of *La Bohème.*

Throughout its long history the Theater an der Wien has been subject to modifications, the most significant of which took place in 1900 when a four-story apartment house was constructed on the Linke Wienzeile aspect. The main entrance is now on the ground floor of this building.

After severe damage to the Staatsoper in the closing days of the Second World War, the Theater an der Wien became the temporary home of the State Opera Company, a duty it shared with the Volksoper until 1954.

By 1960 this theatre, with its rich and diverse musical history, had become redundant and demolition was a serious possibility. At the last moment the City of Vienna authorities purchased the theatre and arranged for complete modernisation. Today it is used principally for musicals. But once a year it becomes the home of the Vienna festival and opera is once again heard here.

B   The Vienna State Opera (Staatsoper)

The Vienna State Opera is the flagship of Austrian culture and is ranked in the top four opera houses of the world. But from the very first, this house, both the building and the institution, has been the subject of continuous controversy.

The building was constructed between 1861 and 1869 as part of the Ringstrasse urban renewal project. The existing Court theatre devoted to opera, the Kärntnertor theatre, was cramped, outmoded and inadequate and, rich in musical history though it was, replacement was necessary.

The design for the new opera house was put out to tender. The winners were the architects Eduard van der Nüll and August Sicard von Sicardsburg who had based their design on Palladio's Basilica in Vicenza.

The critics became vociferous even before the shell of the building was completed. It was to the Emperor Franz Josef himself that the most damning remark was attributed: "The building appears to be sinking into the ground". Such was the vitriol directed towards the two architects that neither lived to see the inauguration of their opera house; Van der Nüll committed suicide and Sicardsburg suffered a fatal heart attack two months later.

The new Hofoper opened in May 1869 with a performance of Mozart's *Don Giovanni*. The antipathy of the Viennese to the exterior did not extend to the interior which received universal acclamation. The tasteful décor of the foyer and the loggia, was much admired.

During its first decade the Hofoper witnessed **Verdi** conducting *Aida* and his "Requiem Mass", **Wagner** directing *Lohengrin* and **Brahms** conducting his "German Requiem".

The list of directors of the Vienna Opera is remarkable; it includes Richter, Mahler, Richard Strauss, Clemens Krauss, Weingartner, von Karajan, Böhm, Maazel and Abbado. The position of Director of the Vienna Opera is perhaps the most coveted in the world of music, but it has so often proved to be a poisoned chalice. So many of the world's great conductors have arrived with high hopes and aspirations only to resign amid acrimony and recriminations sooner rather than later.

The reign of **Gustav Mahler,** director between 1897 and 1907, is regarded as the golden age of opera in Vienna, but it proved to be a tempestuous period. Mahler arrived in Vienna determined to rid the company of "slovenliness". He dismissed singers and players that he considered to be below standard and appointed replacements. Mahler involved himself in all aspects of opera, including lighting and designing. He appointed the secessionist Alfred Roller as designer, although Roller had no previous experience, with brilliant results. During performances Mahler also insisted on the house lights being dimmed and refused admission to latecomers until a suitable interval.

Mahler's ruthless drive for perfection raised artistic standards dramatically, but also made him many enemies. Before long there were whispering campaigns in the press prompted by anti-Semitism and Mahler was forced to resign through sheer exhaustion.

There was fierce opposition to **Richard Strauss** even before he was appointed in 1919 as co-director with Franz Schalk. Opponents cited his lack of experience of running an opera house and fears that Strauss would swamp the schedules with his own works, which at that time were not highly regarded in Vienna. Strauss took over at a difficult time. After the end of the First World War the Habsburg Empire had collapsed and Vienna became the capital of the small country of Austria. The Hofoper became the Staatsoper at a time when the national economy was in difficulty and the currency devalued. In the event the only world première of Strauss's works during his tenure were *Die Frau ohne Schatten* and his frivolous ballet *Schlagobers*. By 1924 the complaints familiar to so many directors in Vienna were being levelled at Strauss: the cost of productions and the number of conducting engagements elsewhere. Strauss was asked to submit his resignation.

In 1945, ironically after a performance of *Götterdämmerung*, the building was struck by a bomb. The auditorium and stage area were totally destroyed. The foyer, the loggia, the Imperial Tea Salon and the main staircase survived, although with severe heat damage. During the ten-year rebuilding of the Staatsoper performances were given at the Theater an der Wien and the Volksoper.

The destruction of the rear of the house gave an opportunity to install modern stage machinery. Today the stages and their machinery, including computerised electrical and hydraulic systems, are the envy of most of the world's opera houses.

After the re-opening of the house in 1955, Vienna enjoyed a second "golden age". **Herbert von Karajan** become director in 1956, a post he held for ten years. Karajan, even more of a control freak than Mahler, presided over a glittering but tempestuous period of the history of the Staatsoper. He insisted that all operas be performed in the language in which they were written and not in an inadequate translation. He negotiated an enormous subsidy from the Austrian government and brought to Vienna singers of the calibre of Leontyre Price, Tebaldi, Freni, di Stefano and Gobbi. He also persuaded **Stravinsky** to conduct a performance of *Oedipus Rex*.

Even with a huge state subsidy, Karajan's financial demands resulted in a large budget deficit. After a disagreement Karajan resigned leaving the Staatsoper with an international reputation second to none but with greatly depleted coffers.

When **Lorin Maazel** was appointed director in 1984 the Staatsoper secured the services of not only a fine conductor but also a gifted and experienced musical administrator. Maazel tried to put the house on a sound financial footing by introducing the "block system" whereby an operatic production would be given a number of performances during a short period of time, each with the same conductor and cast. This would replace the haphazard arrangement whereby performances were given at irregular periods with different casts. But the Viennese, obdurately conservative as ever, were unhappy. Before long the critics were carping in the press and the inevitable resignation was in the post.

In essence the task of the Director of the Vienna State Opera is an impossible one and it is one of the mysteries of the world of music that so many distinguished conductors allow themselves to be persuaded to take it on.

The causes of successive directors' difficulties are probably twofold: firstly that Vienna is an opera-obsessed city and, secondly, the large state subsidy gives all Viennese tax-payers a proprietorial interest in the Staatsoper. There are few Viennese who do not believe that they would make a better director than the current incumbent.

Operatic performances at the Staatsoper are usually sold out. Visitors are advised to apply for tickets at least three weeks before the performance. The box office is at the Bunderstheaterkasen at Goethegasse 1 A1010 Wien. The fax number is 51444-2969.

Occasionally, on the day of the performance, returns are available but often the only recourse is to the ticket agencies which usually have tickets available although with a significant surcharge.

Tickets are not inexpensive, but for the impecunious there are the celebrated "stehplatz" (standing places), of which there are no less 550. Queuing for a long time may be necessary, but the reward is to watch a performance at the Staatsoper for a fraction of the price of a seat.

On most days, rehearsals permitting, guided tours of the Staatsoper are available in a number of languages.

XXI The Musikverein and the Konzerthaus

A   The Musikverein

Although "the building of the Society of Friends of Music in Vienna" (Gesellschaft der Musikfreunde in Wien) is the prosaic official name of one of Vienna's most familiar landmarks, it is known universally as the Musikverein.

The Society was founded in 1812 by a group of music-lovers, many of whom were accomplished musicians. The economic consequences of the Napoleonic wars had reduced the traditional patrons of music, the aristocracy, to penury and the emerging middle-class took responsibility to protect and promote music in all its facets.

For many years the Society's headquarters were in cramped rooms in the Tuchlauben (see IV: 10). When the Ringstrasse and its associated new buildings were in the planning stage in the middle of the nineteenth century, Emperor Franz Josef gave permission to the Society to construct a new building opposite the Karlskirche. Theophil Hansen was commissioned to design the building. After a construction period of three years the new building was completed in 1870 and its clean neo-classical design instantly won favour with the Viennese.

The principal function of the Society was to give a series of concerts each year. One of the first directors of these concerts was **Johannes Brahms** who held the post of Director of the Society's concerts from 1872 until 1875. At one of these concerts Brahms introduced the orchestral version of his "Variations on the St Anthony Chorale". The last conductor to hold the position of director was **Herbert von Karajan**.

The society also founded a conservatory of music. **Bruckner** was a member of the academic staff and **Mahler, Wolf** and **Zemlinsky** spent their student days here. Early in the twentieth century the conservatory outgrew the rooms allocated and the society handed on the responsibility to the Austrian government.

The departure of the conservatory released a number of rooms which were subsequently occupied by prestigious tenants. These included the piano-makers Bösendorfer and the violin manufacturer Lang. The most famous tenant is the Vienna Philharmonic Orchestra which enjoys a symbiotic relationship with the Society, which has no professional orchestra of its own.

The Vienna Philharmonic Orchestra

To become a member of the Vienna Philharmonic Orchestra it is necessary to have been engaged by the Vienna State Opera for at least three years. The VPO is a self-governing orchestra administrated by a committee of twelve, elected by the whole orchestra. Since 1933 it has had no permanent conductor and engages its conductors on a guest basis. The orchestra gives a series of concerts each year, the most famous being the New Year's Day concert which is watched by one billion television viewers worldwide.

The orchestra's concerts are traditionally given at 4pm on Saturday and at 11am on Sunday which emphasises its dual rôle.

The Society's concerts have been taken over by the city's second world class orchestra, the Vienna Symphony, which plays at most of the Society's concerts.

Over the years the Society has accumulated an astonishing collection of valuable scores, books and mementos which are held in the Society's archives. There are items from all the great composers. The original scores of Mozart's Piano Concerto No. 20 in D minor and the Symphony No. 40 in G minor together with Beethoven's score of the "Eroica Symphony", with the title page defaced by the composer, are among the treasures held here in a carefully controlled environment, with temperature and humidity constantly monitored. Both Brahms and von Einem bequeathed their musical scores to the Society. Thus the former's "German Requiem" is held here.

Occasional exhibitions are held and the archives are available to scholars on Monday, Wednesday and Friday mornings.

The crowning glory of the Musikverein is the "Grosser Musikvereinssaal". To enter the Great Hall is a stunning experience.

The décor is sumptuous with gold predominating. The aesthetics are complemented by the superb acoustics of the hall. Acoustics is not an exact science and many have attempted to copy the Great Hall without success. Factors include a suspended ceiling and a "sounding box" below the floor which acts rather like the body of a violin.

The hall holds over 1700 seated and 300 standing. Tickets are always at a premium.

The podium of the Great Hall has been occupied by most of the great musical names of the late nineteenth and twentieth centuries, although not all enjoyed success.

In 1877 **Anton Bruckner** conducted the disastrous first performance of his Third Symphony with the VPO. Bruckner was an incompetent conductor and the orchestra earlier had declared the work to be "unplayable". Thus the portents were unfavourable. Whistling and cat-calls punctuated the performance and the audience then drifted away *en masse*. At the conclusion there were only 25 people remaining, one of whom **Gustav Mahler**, then a 17 year-old student, hastened to console the composer. Bruckner's Symphonies 2 and 4 were also premièred here rather more successfully, perhaps because they were conducted by others.

The second and third symphonies of **Johannes Brahms** also received their first performances here in 1877 and 1887 respectively, both conducted by Hans Richter to great acclaim. Brahms's last appearance in this hall was in March 1897, three weeks before his death from cancer of the liver. Richter conducted the Symphony No 4 in E minor and there were emotional scenes as Brahms, emaciated and deeply jaundiced, acknowledged the ovation and bade farewell to Vienna.

When Brahms's third symphony was premièred here in 1883, the programme also included the first Viennese performance of the Violin Concerto by **Antonin Dvořák** in the presence of the composer. Dvořák, regarded by the Viennese as a protégée of Brahms, was always a popular visitor to the Musikverein. Dvořák sat with Brahms in the Director's box for the first Viennese performance of the "Symphony from the New World" which was a sensation.

Tchaikowsky never found favour among the Viennese; when the first performance of his Violin Concerto was given in the Golden Hall in 1881 there was uproar. The critics, led by Eduard Hanslick, were vituperative in their reviews. Hansick declared that in this concerto, now standard repertoire, "the violin is torn apart, beaten black and blue; the music stinks". Fortunately the composer was not in Vienna for the performance.

Richard Wagner, on the other hand, had brilliant successes when he conducted concerts of his own music in the Golden Hall in 1872 and 1875. Wagner was raising money for his new theatre at Bayreuth.

The New Year's Day concerts in this hall have distinguished antecedents. Just before the inauguration of the new building the Society signed an agreement with **Johann Strauss (son)** for a series of Strauss concerts in the Golden Hall. At the Inaugural Ball, all three Strauss brothers, Johann, Josef and Eduard, conducted new compositions dedicated to the Society.

Between 1898 and 1901 **Gustav Mahler** conducted the subscription concerts of the Vienna Philharmonic Orchestra in this hall. It was not a happy arrangement for either party. Mahler, as director of the Hofoper, had upset the orchestra on a number of occasions when it played in the guise of the house orchestra in the Opera, and after three seasons of mutual antagonism Mahler resigned. Not one of Mahler's symphonies received their premières here. Mahler did conduct the first Viennese performance of his Fourth Symphony, after which a young student, **Alban Berg**, begged Mahler to let him have the baton which the conductor had used. It remained a treasured possession of Berg until his death.

A successor of Mahler at the Opera, **Richard Strauss**, enjoyed a much more amicable relationship with the Vienna Philharmonic Orchestra. Like Mahler, Strauss was a fine conductor and conducted the VPO on many occasions. For its centenary concert, the orchestra invited Strauss to conduct his *Alpensinfonie*.

Another composer who enjoyed a success in this hall was the Norwegian **Edvard Grieg**. He conducted his Piano Concerto here in 1896. The soloist was **Busoni**.

Some of the most memorable (and infamous) concerts in the Golden Hall have been associated with the Second Viennese School, led by Arnold Schoenberg, of which Berg and Webern were leading lights.

Schoenberg conducted the first performance of his *Pelleas und Melisande* in 1905 in this hall. His first major success in Vienna came in 1913 when Franz Schreker conducted the vast and sprawling *Gurrelieder*, after the end of which Schoenberg received an ovation which lasted for half an hour.

But a few weeks later Schoenberg conducted a concert which is referred to by musical historians as the "Skandal-Konzert". The programme was scheduled to include pieces by **Alban Berg, Anton von Webern, Alexander von Zemlinsky, Mahler** and **Schoenberg.**

The audience was a mixture of the committed, the sceptical, the curious and also a large group which had arrived primed to cause trouble.

During the first work on the programme, Webern's Orchestral Pieces (Op 6) there was both applause and hissing. Schoenberg's Chamber Symphony (Op 9) elicited the shrill sound produced by blowing on to door keys. By the time that Berg's *Altenberg-Lieder* (Op 4) were being sung the audience was out of control. Raucous laughter echoed around the hall and the first of several fist-fights erupted in the gallery.

Schoenberg stopped conducting and arranged for the police to be called. The solitary police officer who eventually arrived stood helplessly and advised Schoenberg to abandon the concert. The musicians on stage fled in panic as the platform was stormed. The concert was abandoned and the hall cleared.

The Musikverein also has two smaller halls, the Brahms-Saal (formerly the Kleine Musikvereinssaal) and the Gottfried-von-Einem Saal.

The Small Hall which was renamed the Brahms-Saal in 1937 is a most beautiful setting for chamber music and Lieder-recitals. Accommodating 600 people it is decorated in green, red and gold.

Clara Schumann played at the inaugural concert in 1870. Brahms was a frequent performer here.

In January 1905 **Mahler** gave a Lieder concert in the Small Hall. On the programme were the first performances of his *Kindertotenlieder,* the *Rückert-Lieder,* and four of the *Wünderhorn-Lieder.* Mahler directed the small orchestra.

It was in the Small Hall also that **Schoenberg's** *Verklärte Nacht* was given its first performance by the Rosé group in 1902.

The Gottfried-von-Einem Saal, formerly the Kammer-Saal, was re-opened under its new name in 1996 after extensive refurbishment. It is used for small concerts, lectures and occasionally for recordings.

The Society's reputation for conservatism, was belied at the beginning of the twenty-first century when it announced a major programme of extension. This involved constructing a large hall under the main entrance and several smaller rooms. One room, seating 400 is a concert hall for children and young people in which concerts of jazz and film music and also theatrical productions will be given. Other rooms are for archives, instruments and rehearsal rooms.

For tickets for performances at the Musikverein, the box office address is I Karlsplatz 6, telephone 505 81 90. The Fax no. 505 81 90-94 and the e-mail address is tickets@musikverein.at.

B   Wiener Konzerthaus

Vienna's second major concert hall was built in 1912-13 in Art Nouveau style. The architects were Ferdinand Fellner and Hermann Helmer. There are three halls; the Grosser Saal accommodates over 2000, the Mozart-Saal seats 900 and the Schubert-Saal has a capacity of 400. **Richard Strauss** composed his *Festlischer Präludium* for the official opening in October 1913.

Attached to the Konzerthaus is the Akadamietheater and the Academy of Music and Performing Arts, which had it origins as the Conservatory of the Society of Friends of Music.

The building was commissioned by the Wiener Konzert-Gesellschaft (Vienna Concert Society) which was founded in 1908. For so long music had been the preserve of the aristocracy and the wealthy middle-class. The aim of the Konzert-Verein was to bring music to a much broader spectrum of society. A priority was to establish a new orchestra. Thus there came into being an orchestra which eventually evolved, from 1933, into the Wiener Symphoniker (Vienna Symphony Orchestra).

In order to bring music to new audiences the concert society organised a series of "workers' symphony concerts" which were held in the Grosser Saal from 1913 until 1934. In 1922 **Anton von Webern** was appointed director of these concerts. In 1925 Webern marked the 200th workers' concert by conducting Mahler's gigantic eighth symphony.

Concert programmes at the Konzerthaus have been much more adventurous than those of the Musikverein. There is a strong predilection for contemporary music, in particular by **Schoenberg** and his disciples. **Hindemith** appeared here conducting his *Mathis der Maler* and *Symphonica Serene* and other visitors have included **von Einem** and **William Walton.**

In 1918 **Schoenberg** founded the "Verein für musikalische Privataufführungen (Society for private musical performances). The aim was to provide a forum for contemporary music.

Concerts were held in the Schubertsaal for three years. There were strict rules; there was to be no publicity for the concerts and no applause. In other words only devotees would attend (over 300 members enrolled) and the usual elements of concerts by Schoenberg, hissing, booing and cat-calls, would be absent. The works were usually given in piano reduction, but occasionally a small orchestra would be employed. Schoenberg and Webern were the conductors.

Tickets for concerts at the Konzerthaus are available from the box office at Lothringerstrasse 20, Postfach 140, A-1037 Wien. Telephone: 242 002, Fax: 242 00110.

Principal Sources and Select Bibliography

Anderson, Emily

The letters of Mozart and His Family
New York, 1985

Bär, Carl

Mozart : Krankheit, Tod, Begräbris
Salzburg, 1967

Barea, Ilsa

Vienna : Legend and Reality
London, 1966

Berlioz, Hector

Memoirs (Translated and edited by David
Cairns) London, 1969

Boyden, Matthew

Richard Strauss
London, 1999

Braunbehrens,Volkmar

Mozart in Vienna, 1781-1791
London, 1990

Ed.Cooper, Barry

The Beethoven Compendium
London 1991

Cooper, Martin

Beethoven, The Last Decade, 1871-1827
London, 1970

Deutsch, Otto Erich

Mozart : A Documentary Biography
London, 1990

Schubert : A Documentary Biography
(Trans. E. Blom), London, 1946

de la Grange, Henry-Louis

Gustav Mahler : Vienna, the Years of Challenge
Oxford, 1995

	Gustav Mahler : Vienna, Triumph and Disillusion Oxford, 1999
Hanson, Alice	*Musical life in Biedermeier Vienna* Cambridge, 1985
Kein, Rudolf	*Beethoven Stätten in Österreich* Vienna, 1970
	Schubert Stätten Vienna, 1973
McKay, Elizabeth	*Franz Schubert : A Biography* Oxford, 1996
May, Florence	*The Life of Brahms* (2 vols) New Jersey, 1981
Moldenhauer, Hans	*Anton von Webern, a chronicle of his* *Life and Works* London, 1978
Monson, Karen	*Alban Berg* Boston, 1979
Prawy, Marcel	*The Vienna Opera* London, 1969
Robbins-London, H.C	*Mozart : The Golden Years* London, 1989
	1791 : Mozart's Last Year *London, 1988*

Haydn : His Life and Music (with David Wyn Jones) London, 1988

Schönzeler, Hans-Hubert. *Dvořák*
London, 1984

Schorske, Carl E *Fin de Siècle Vienna.*
London, 1979

Solomon, Maynard *Beethoven*
New York, 1977

Specht, Richard *Johannes Brahms*
(Trans.E.Blom), Glasgow, 1930.

Stuckenschmidt, H.H *Arnold Schoenberg : His Life, World and Work*
(Trans.H.Searle), London, 1977

Thayer, A.W *Life of Beethoven.*
(Ed.Forbes), Princeton, 1964

Walker, Frank *Hugo Wolf*
London, 1951

Wechsberg, Joseph *The Waltz Emperors*
London, 1973

Index

Albrechtsberger	*II:5, VI:12, XVII A*
Bartók	*XIII:1*
Beethoven	*II:3, II:11, II:12, II:16, II:17,*
	II:19, II:24, II:25, III:6, III:8,
	IV:5, IV:9, IV:25, IV:26, IV:30,
	IV:31, IV:32, V:1C, V:1G, V:1I,
	V:6, V:7, V:27, V:29, VI:16, VI:20,
	VII:5, VII:6, VII:10, VII:12,
	VII:14, VIII:13, X:5, XI:13, XI:14,
	XI:24, XII:3, XII:10, XII:11,
	XII:12, XIII:3, XIV:5, XIV:6,
	XIV:7, XIV:9, XV:5, XV:8, XV:9,
	XV:10, XV:11, XVI:2, XVI:5,
	XVII:B, XVIII: A4, XVIII:A5,
	XVIII:A7, XVIII:A8, XVIII:A9,
	XVIII:A10, XVIII:A11, XVIII:
	A12, XVIII:C, XIX:C, XIX:D,
	XX:A
Berg	*IV:8, V:17, VII:18, VIII:16, XI:3,*
	XVI:8, XVI:10, XVI:16, XVI:18,
	XXI:A
Berlioz	*V:1C, V:1G, XX:A*
Brahms	*II:2, III:6, III:10, IV:10, V:1G,*
	V:7, V:17, V:26, VI:19, VI:20,
	VII:9, VII:13, VIII:7, VIII:14,
	IX:3, IX:15, X:6, X:11, XII:4,
	XVII:B, XX:B, XXI:A
Bruckner	*II:23, III:8, IV:22, IV:28, V:2,*
	V:15, V:26, VII:21, VIII:5, IX:15,

	XI:17, XII:15, XII:17, XIII:3, XXI:A
Busoni	XIV:10, XXI:A
Chopin	I, V:1G, V:22
Cimarosa	V:1C
Dittersdorf	XI:22
Donizetti	V:7
Dvořák	V:1B, IX:8, XXI:A
von Einem	II:13, XXI:A
Enescu	IX:4
Eybler	VI:12
Eysler	VIII:15, XI:15, XII:2, XV:3, XVII:B
Flotow	V:7, XIX:A3
Foerster	XVI:15
Fux	I, III:16, IV:27, V:1F, V:12
Gluck	V:1C, V:1F, V:1G, VIII:6, IX:9, XI:22, XVII:B
Goldmark	VII:1, IX:15, XII:6, XVII:B
Grieg	II:9, XXI:A
Haydn	I, II:18, II:19, II:20, II:24, III:3, III:8, IV:20, IV:23, IV:28, IV:29, V:1C, V:1G, V:1I, V:6, V:8, V:9, V:20, V:23, VI:9, X:1, X:10, X:11, X:14, X:17, XVI:3A, XVI:3C
Hellmesberger	III:5
Herbeck	III:16, V:1F, XI:17
Kálmán	IX:5, IX:11, XII:5

Korngold	*XIII:2*
Kreisler	*VI:5*
Kreutzer	*VI:6, XI:4*
Lanner	*IV:4, V:1G, VI:10 VI:20, VI:23, X:2, X:8, XI:1, XI:6, XI:7, XIV:1, XIV:4, XVII:B, XVIII:A1*
Lehár	*V:15, VI:23, X:3, X:6, XI:3, XV:12, XX:A*
Liszt	*IV:28, V:1G, X:5*
Lortzing	*IX:12, XX:A*
Mahler	*II:26, V:15, V:26, VI:23, VII:16, VIII:3, VIII:5, IX:7, X:12, XI:20, XII:7, XIV:3, XIV:11, XV:1, XV:6, XV:7, XVI:13, XX:B, XXI:A*
Millöcker	*X:7, XVII:B, XX:A*
Mozart	*I, II:2, II:9, II:10, II:14, II:16, II:24, III:4, III:6, III:12, IV:1, IV:3, IV:7, IV:12, IV:13, IV:14, IV:16, IV:17, IV:18, IV:19, IV:21, IV:22, IV:24, IV:29, IV:30, V:1A, V:1C, V:1D, V:1G, V:1I, V:4, V:5, V:10, V:18, V:21, V:24, V:25, VI:16, VII:4, VII:11, VII:19, IX:6, XI:9, XI:17, XI:22, XII:16, XVI:3A, XVI:3B, XVI:3C, XVII: A, XVIII:A2, XVIII:A3*
Nicolai	*II:21*
Offenbach	*VI:23, VII:3, XX:A*
Paganini	*V:1G*
Puccini	*VI:23, IX:15, XX:A*

Rossini	*XX:A*
Rubinstein	*V:26, XIV:10*
Salieri	*II:1, V:1F, V:14, XII:9, XVII:B, XVIII:A9*
Schmidt	*XVI:13, XVII:B, XVIII:B*
Schoenberg	*V:17, V:19, V:26,VI:1, VI:13, VI:14, VI:18,VI:20, VI:23, VII:17, VII:18, VIII:11, XI:23,XIII:6, XIII:11, XVI:9, XVI:14, XVII:B, XVIII:C, XXI:A, XXI:B*
Schubert	*II:3, II:4, II:7, II:12, II:14, II:23, III:4, III:7, III:9, IV:4, IV:6, IV:10, IV:11, IV:15, IV:18, IV:26, IV:28, IV:30, IV:31, V:2, V:13, V:27, VI:12, VI:15, VI:16, VII:7, VIII:10, IX:9, IX:14, X:9, X:10, XI:6, XI:10, XI:19, XII:1, XII:9, XII:10, XII:18, XII:19, XIII:3, XIII:4, XIII:5, XIII:7, XIII:8, XIII:9, XIII:10, XIV:6,*
	XV:4, XVII:B, XVIII:A6, XIX:A2, XIX:B, XX:A
Schumann	*III:11, XIII:3*
Sechter	*II:22, VI:11, XI:17*
Sibelius	*IX:10*
Stolz	*VIII:2, IX:5, X:13, XI:19, XV:2, XVI:11, XVII:B, XX:A*
Straus	*VI;2, VI:23*
Strauss (Eduard)	*VI:6, VI:8, XI:21*
Strauss (Johann, father)	*I, III:2, IV:4, V:1G, V:30, VI:4,*

	VI:10, VI:20, VIII:14, X:2, XI:1, XI:8, XIII:9, XIV:4, XVII:B, XVIII:A1
Strauss (Johann, son)	I, II:6, V:17, V:30, VI:6, VI:15, VI:16, VI:20, VI:21, VI:23, VI:24, VII:3, VIII:4, VIII:5, IX:15, XI:3, XI:6, XI:8, XI:12, XI:14, XI:19, XIV:8, XVI:7, XVI:11 XVI:17, XVII:B, XVIII:A6, XIX:A1, XX:A, XXI:A
Strauss (Josef)	VI:7, VI:8, VI:15, VI:22, VII:3, VIII:4, XVII:A XVII:B
Strauss (Richard)	II:15, VII:154, VII:20, XX:B, XXI:B
Suppé	III:14, V:2, VI:3, VI:23, VIII:1, IX:13, XI:14, XI:17, XVII:B, XX:A
Szymanowski	IX:2
Vivaldi	I, VIII:4
Voříšek	V:1F, XII:9
Wagner	II:8, IV:26, VI:16, VIII:9, XI:11, XV1:6, XX:A, XX:B,
Weber	II:14, IV:9, V:7, XVIII:A5, XVIII:A9
Webern	VII:2, VII:18, VIII:3, XII:13, XIII:6, XIV:12, XV1:1, XV1:12, XVIII:C, XXI:A, XXI:B
Wittgenstein	XV:1
Wolf	III:1, V:11, IX:1, XI:16, XII:8, XII:14, XIV:2, XVI:18, XVII:B, XVIII:B, XXI:A
Zemlinsky	V:15, V:19, VI:14, VI:23, XIII:6, XX:A, XXI:A
Ziehrer	V:1G, V:15, VI:6, VII:8, XI:2